Politics and Prejudice
Small-town Blacks Battle a Corrupt System

By Richard E. Harris

Changing Outlook Press

Media, Pennsylvania

© 2008 Richard E. Harris
Published by Changing Outlook Press, an imprint of Changing Outlook LLC.
ISBN: 978-0-9816504-1-8

This is a revised edition of the book entitled *Politics and Prejudice: A history of Chester (PA) Negroes*, published in 1991 by Relmo Publishers.

> We welcome your comments and suggestions. Please send them to:
> Changing Outlook Press
> 437 East Franklin Street
> Media, PA 19063
>
> or email them to:
> george@changingoutlook.com.

Cover photograph by Jack T. Franklin, courtesy of the African American Museum in Philadelphia.

Cover quote is from *Organized Crime in Pennsylvania: A Decade of Change. 1990 Report.* Commonwealth of Pennsylvania, 1990.

To the memory of all the
Black journalists I have
known and worked with
across the nation over
the past 50 years

Richard E. Harris was born on the Eastern Shore of Maryland in 1912. He began his career as a volunteer youth and recreation worker in Pennsylvania, later becoming a journalist for a variety of newspapers, including 12 Black papers from across the country. He has interviewed numerous well known figures, including W.E.B. DuBois, Dr. Emmett J. Scott, Ethel Waters, Mayor Tom Bradley, Supreme Court Justice Thurgood Marshall, and singer-activist Paul Robeson.

As a crusading reporter, he was on the front lines of the Chester civil rights struggles of the 1940s, when he began Chester's first Black newspaper, *The Crusader*. *The Crusader* became a driving force behind Chester's post-war desegregation battles. A Chester resident for over two decades, Harris was a witness to much of what he describes in *Politics and Prejudice*.

He later moved to Arizona, where he joined the staff of the *Arizona Republic*. Subsequently, he worked for many years for the Phoenix Urban League. He was a central figure in organizing the George Washing Carver Museum and Cultural Center in Phoenix, and has also been an important sponsor of scholarships for Black youth.

Other books by Richard E. Harris:
Delinquency in our Democracy, 1954
Black Heritage in Arizona, 1977
The First Hundred Years: A History of Arizona Blacks, 1983
The Gift of Estevan, Black Comrade of Conquistadores, 1999
The American Odyssey of a Black Journalist, 2003

Contents

Foreword 6

Introduction 9

Chapter 1 15
Some Came Sooner Than William Penn

Chapter 2 29
Political Machine Gears Up (1910-25)

Chapter 3 39
South Chester, A Thriving Community (1926-35)

Chapter 4 57
Segregated Schools Finally Targeted (1936-40)

Chapter 5 67
War Years Create A Boom-Town (1941-45)

Chapter 6 82
Postwar Era Sparks Civic Awakening (1946-50)

Chapter 7 102
Town Undergoes Strange Metamorphosis (1951-60)

Chapter 8 114
New Black Leadership Cadre Emerges (1961-70)

Chapter 9 128
The Controversial John Nacrelli Decade (1971-80)

Chapter 10 144
First Black Woman Appointed Mayor (1981-90)

EPILOGUE 162

APPENDIX 169

Index 172

Contributions of Richard E. Harris 186

Foreword

Chester, Pennsylvania, is a small city on the banks of the Delaware River not far from Philadelphia. On the surface, it seems to be simply one more representative of the industrial centers that thrived after World War II and then sank into decay. It lost population as its industrial base withered. Once overwhelmingly white, its white residents fled to suburbs and the city gradually became overwhelmingly Black. Chester, once the retail center for a large area between Philadelphia and Wilmington, Delaware, found many of its stores closing as the new suburban malls drew customers away. Unemployment grew, at one point becoming the highest in Pennsylvania.

That is how Chester looked to the outside world, and to the white residents who left. But how did it look from the inside? How did the Black population of Chester see these changes?

Chester is fortunate to have exactly the right person to tell that side of its story. Richard E. Harris is a Black journalist who lived in Chester during a key period in its history and who published a newspaper there for a time. Harris is able to provide an insider's perspective on the long and sometimes bloody struggle for the desegregation of nearly every aspect of Chester, from its lunch counters and theaters to its schools, jobs, and housing. It is a story that involves a host of nationally-famous players, including Malcolm X, Dick Gregory, and Martin Luther King, Jr., among many others.

At the same time as Chester's Blacks were struggling for their basic rights, they had to contend with an utterly corrupt political machine. Under the control of white bosses (but with Blacks gradually taking on important roles as well) the machine ruled Chester with an iron fist for many decades. Ultimately, many of the worst offenders ended up in Federal prison. This, too, is a story Harris tells.

Harris was also able to gather information about the earlier history of Blacks in Chester, including, for example, the fact that there

Foreword

were Black slaves in Chester before William Penn ever set foot on North American soil.

Richard Harris published his description of the still-unfinished odyssey of Chester's Black population in 1991, in a remarkable book called *Politics and Prejudice: A History of Chester (PA) Negroes*. It sold well locally, but eventually went out of print. Harris had long since settled in Arizona.

That was where matters stood until 2007, when one of us (Janet) came across a copy of *Politics and Prejudice*. She immediately recognized its importance. In her job as archivist for Chester-based Widener University, she had found it difficult to find good material on Chester's post-war history, and *Politics and Prejudice* was a treasure-trove of material about that period, as well as a source for the neglected history of Chester Blacks that stretches back to pre-revolutionary times.

Her excitement prompted the other one of us (George) to become interested in publishing a new edition of the book. Being familiar with book publishing and the recent changes in printing technology, George saw that it might be practical to bring the book back into print, and together we began working on the project. Thanks to the internet, Janet was able to track down Richard Harris (now in his 90s) in Arizona, and he agreed to the new edition.

We then began the editorial work and production process: scanning the text, proofreading and editing it, finding new photos where possible, laying out the book, and creating a new index. In the process, we have kept the changes to a minimum. We have primarily made minor text changes to correct typographic errors and to improve readability. We have substituted photos in instances where we have been able to obtain pictures that are better than we could get by simply re-scanning those of the original book.

Two significant changes were made in consultation with Richard Harris. The first was a change in the book's subtitle. Harris suggested changing it to "Small-town Blacks battle a corrupt system," reflecting the fact that the book is of interest to anyone interested in Black urban history, not just to those interested in Chester's history. The other change was to use "Blacks" throughout the book, except in direct quotes. (The original version had used "Negroes" and "colored" at various points, reflecting the time period being discussed; that usage now seems dated.)

In a few cases, especially in the Appendix, we have added data to tables to bring them up to date. Although the data was not in the original edition of the book, we think readers will be interested in seeing how Chester has been changing in recent years.

And how is Chester doing? The answer is mixed. There are some positive signs—for example, the population is no longer dropping, there is much new housing, and there are good examples of new, thriving small businesses—but the school system and the retail sector are still struggling, and there are many other problems to be overcome. Still, Chester is making progress. Anyone who doubts it need only read this book to see how far Chester residents have come by taking matters into their own hands, overcoming one obstacle after another. That process continues today.

Janet and George Alexander, Editors

October, 2008

Introduction

Chester is the oldest city in Pennsylvania, and the place where thousands from across the seas fled to escape religious and political persecution. Yet many of their descendents soon established patterns of racial prejudice and discrimination against Black people. William Penn, proprietor of the new area, perhaps established in the minds of his compatriots ideas contributing to the low esteem of Blacks already living there as slaves. He once remarked, for instance, that slaves were more valuable and lasting than the indentured white servants.

Later, as slaves or freedmen began migrating—many from the comparatively mild-mannered clime of Maryland's eastern shores, they became pawns in a political atmosphere that would relegate them to second-class citizenship for generations hence.

Since that period, a great many contradictions and paradoxes about the city and its history seem in dire need of exploration or explanations in order to gain some insights into matters relating especially to its Black citizens.

Once in the deceptively friendly confines of Chester, the Black population increased gradually between 1870 and 1915. Under the leadership of former slaves or their offspring, they proceeded to establish their own society, organizing churches, lodges and businesses. In doing so, were they unconsciously beginning to form their own patterns of segregation? Of course, in a broad sense, this represented safety in numbers. The abolitionist-minded Quakers, demonstrating their paternalistic spirit, did further—consciously or not—help draw tighter those racial lines. They lent helping hands in community organizing and sponsored a few institutions of higher learning for the Blacks, and others for whites, the most notable in the area being the exclusive Swarthmore College.

During this pre-1900 era, Blacks in other areas of the nation were entering prestigious colleges, yet in Chester there was only one case of note; Thomas M. Thomas graduated from Lincoln University in nearby Oxford, Pennsylvania. That institution was founded by the Presbyterians, another liberal religious domination; and under their banner Mr. Thomas built a church in 1898, serving as pastor and community leader.

As the Blacks gradually established themselves, their neighborhoods were generally surrounded by not-too-friendly factions, tending to restrict their opportunities for socioeconomic pursuits. A short distance from the city borders lay the Main Line sections where the captains of industry and other well-heeled families resided. Adjacent to the city's north and south boundaries and along the Delaware River sat large industrial concerns offering minimal labor inducements. At the lower end of their predominant south Chester neighborhood were located those residents of Eastern Europen descent whose language and culture kept them apart not only from Blacks but numerous white Americans as well. Indeed, fear of the "unknown" could be made applicable to each of these groups, stimulating mistrust and animosity.

Such existing conditions could invariably play into the hands of ambitious, devious-minded individuals anxious to "divide and conquer" for political or economic purposes. Yet in such a situation, one might be tempted to ask how could a political schemer, for instance, manage to keep three diverse factions so far apart until election days, when all would unquestionably support the same candidates and causes?

The public school system's operation provided a prime example of the political forces' manipulation of the citizenry. Numerous school buildings set aside for Blacks were often located mere city blocks from those designated for whites. Despite state laws against public school segregation, local authorities allowed the practice to persist. In earlier times, it was apparently no difficult matter for authorities to convince Black leaders that their qualified teachers could be hired only if they agreed to teach segregated classes. In their area, residents of foreign descent operated under similar arrangements.

This town, like others across the nation, became the scene of violent race riots around the period of the first World War. In some cities, the hatred lay so deep-seated, it exploded from a single Black-white fight, or from a wild, false rumor, as bitter rivalry existed

Introduction

between migrating southern whites and urban Blacks over jobs in war industries. Regarding the Chester riots, Blacks held only the lowest-paying jobs—which untrained newcomer whites evidently craved. Authorities in some cities either ignored the besieged Blacks or secretly encouraged white rioters. The role Chester officials performed in the local conflagrations turned out to be a most interesting one.

While great masses of Blacks began leaving the South seeking improved domestic as well as physical security, it seemed that only a small percentage of the migrants chose Chester as their new home, possibly because this relatively small town seemed a more convenient refuge than such an urban metropolis as, say, the nearby "City of Brotherly Love." However, Chester's Black population did increase substantially during and after the Second World War, even though the economic and social state of affairs could be considered equivalent to that of a modern southern town where segregation was a way of life, and only whites held public offices.

In fact, whether or not the new migrants knew it, Chester was virtually ruled by a political machine easily compared to the Crump syndicate in Memphis. The question, then, might be asked why the citizens of the oldest city in a northern state could be controlled by the McClure political oligarchy long after other Blacks across the county had switched their traditional GOP allegiance to the Democrats at the beginning of the FDR administration in the early 1930s.

There is no doubt that Blacks were not numerous enough earlier to help form a decisive bloc with certain dissatisfied whites and Democrats to challenge the machine, yet even after the second war when their population reached one-third of the city's total, the machine remained supreme. The Blacks' unquestionable contributions to the war effort through industrial and military manpower carried no weight as they continued seeking relief from the burdens of racial restrictions.

The V.J. Day that marked the close of the second war was also— to the surprise of many—the precise time when a small cadre of Black parents launched an attack on segregated and inferior school facilities. Significantly, this action preceded by a generation the nationwide civil rights crusades. Local conservative leadership—civic and political—naturally looked askance on the action. The young instigators, unfortunately, had wrongly anticipated support from among the thousands that had moved to the city for defense jobs. Had the newcomers, many college-bred, reached such a stage of self-satisfaction with their new-found financial status that they decided not to become involved? Or had others with leadership potential moved back to their own home town, or to seemingly more attractive environs—Philadelphia, for instance? To the complete surprise of nearly everyone except their small band of supporters, they eventually won their court case against neighborhood school segregation and public accommodation restrictions.

Evidently realizing they were trailing many other cities in matters of racial progress, the new generation of the Sixties finally launched a full-scale civil rights onslaught. By this time, the local Black population was beginning to equal that of whites, largely through such social phenomena as "white flight" and the emergence of the "baby boomers" born of Black parents during the last war. Moreover, some of those parents, as well as grandparents who were veterans of the last campaign, proudly joined the fray. The community had obviously undergone a complete metamorphosis in its manner of thinking and action. Having consistently ignored outsiders offering their particular brand of leadership, the Black community, in general, now accepted a charismatic newcomer and several young professionals as their guiding lights.

Throughout this campaign aimed at reforms—first in education, then housing, police and hiring practices—the timely visits from such national civil rights giants as Malcolm X, Dick Gregory, Gloria Richardson and James Farmer helped to embolden the protesters' maneuvering determination. Within a year or so of continual agitations, Black residents, supported by some activist white adults and college students, won victories in both the streets and courts, albeit at the costs of jailings and beatings by law enforcement minions. Included among the victims were hundreds of juveniles, the prime intended beneficiaries of the campaign. When the entire public school system was ordered desegregated,

Introduction

numerous new plants replaced deteriorating buildings; included was a new $22 million state-of-the-art high school. Despite the obvious reforms, a puzzling question needing a logical explanation was why—a few semesters later—did Blacks account for such an alarming proportion of high school absences and dropouts.

The eventful aftermath of the overall campaigns for equality and respect eventually evolved into some curious paradoxical events, specifically during the two subsequent decades. A few Blacks were appointed, and later elected, to policy-making positions yet could wield little or no influence. Almost simultaneously industries and businesses were abandoning the city, causing extreme joblessness and heavy welfare rolls. The mayor, successor to the deceased political boss who had reigned for fifty years, was convicted and sent to prison on corruption charges. His brief replacement soon turned his chair over to the first Black mayor, a female. Was the machine at long last showing its appreciation for the long-suffering fidelity of its Black camp followers? Or did it see the handwriting on the wall, being scribbled by the new generation now representing over 60 percent of the electorate?

This historical documentation, nonetheless, seeks to objectively ascertain what bearing episodes of the past hundred years or so had on the present—and invariably the future—human fortunes of Chester's Black citizens.

Over the years, unfortunately, there has been a paucity of studies on Chester, and particularly its minority population. Consequently, most of the later material and knowledge for this book had to be garnered from periodic news reports and census statistics. Many of the late-stage personal interviews came from veteran grass-roots leaders who lived through various periods of change. Regretfully, the same cooperation did not come from local authorities, most being "unavailable." Could fear or caution have motivated such reluctance? By coincidence, a controversy between the county attorney's office and the State Crime Commission was going on to decide whose responsibility it was to further investigate the possibility of an alleged Mafia-connected crime ring being operated in Chester. Local crime statistics could only be culled from the Department of Justice's annual Uniform Crime

Report. And only through correspondence with the Department of Education in Harrisburg could any necessary data on the overhauled local school system be obtained.

Whatever reasons the authorities had for making data "unavailable", the author's credentials could not possibly have been a bar to gathering information normally available from public officials. As an early-on community activist, and later a journalist, he was witness to much of this history for more than two decades. From the mid-1930s to the end of 1950, he worked as either a reporter or editor for such publications as the daily *Chester Times*, the *Crusader*, the Philadelphia editions of the *Afro-American*, the *Pittsburgh Courier* and the *Independent*. During his hiatus from Pennsylvania, he worked for newspapers in Cleveland and Los Angeles, where he wrote *Delinquency In Our Democracy*, a seven-city study of youth problems. In Phoenix, he was religion editor for the *Arizona Republic*. Later he wrote *The First 100 Years—A History of Arizona Blacks*.

Chapter 1

Some Came Sooner Than William Penn

QUAKERS WERE PIONEER ABOLITIONISTS;
EX-SLAVES ORGANIZE COMMUNITIES

The roots of African-American families in eastern Pennsylvania run much deeper than many other ethnic groups that eventually dominated them and stymied their progress. Decades before William Penn received his proprietary grant in 1682 from the English king, people of African heritage had been living in and around present-day Chester, located on the Delaware River's west bank, 14 miles exactly from both Philadelphia and Wilmington, Delaware.

In 1662 the Dutch West Indies Company, which engaged in the slave trade, brought fifty Africans to serve as laborers along the river. Yet compared to the plight of slavery in a few adjacent areas, that in Pennsylvania might be considered a mild institution. Few citizens owned more than two Black slaves who often worked alongside their masters on family farms or in small shops. Many German and Swedish immigrants began joining the Quakers, or Society of Friends, in the campaign for the abolition of slavery.[1]

Under pressure from the Germantown Quakers, the state assembly passed a law in 1711 preventing further importation of slavery in the province, but that law was repealed later by the English government under urging of the Royal African Company. Many Whigs liberated their slaves as the Revolutionary War was being fought to gain the American colonies freedom from England. However, state law in 1780 called for the gradual abolition of serfdom. Under the act, children born of slaves in that year became automatically free at age 28. By 1810 there remained only seven slaves among the 822 Blacks in Chester and surrounding Delaware County.[2]

No doubt, the more liberal environment in Pennsylvania beckoned both fugitive slaves and free families inside its borders, particularly many from Maryland.[3] The lot of free Blacks in that state was, in a sense, as bad as that of the slaves. So repressive were the laws that a freedman could be jailed for being "idle" or "indigent," a situation often resulting from excessive slave labor. Also, there were restrictions against secret societies, religious services[4] except at certain hours, or operating a business. Some freedmen could be threatened with return to slavery if they returned to the state, even to visit relatives. In the aftermath of the Nat Turner episode in 1830 and the John Brown raids on Maryland in 1859, authorities expressed deathly fear that free Blacks were inducing slaves to revolt.[5]

All the while numerous runaway slaves reached Chester through the Underground Railroad, the system utilized by abolitionists to spirit bondsmen out of the South, and which operated way stations in Delaware County.[6] More than a few of these "passengers" from nearby Delaware and the Chesapeake area of Maryland decided to seek their habitats in areas made more livable by Quaker influence. One event illustrating an intense desire to stay in Chester occurred on March 17, 1857 during a bloody incident when ten professional slave-catchers attempted to capture twelve absconding slaves and return them to their masters. But the defenders of their new-found freedom turned on their would-be enslavers; and after a ferocious fight, the bounty hunters quickly retreated southward, empty-handed.[7]

Delaware, once a part of Pennsylvania and with but a few Quakers and abolitionists, became more and more identified with the southern states. Thus the northward trails for fugitive slaves were extremely difficult.

Primarily due to a downturn in their economy, most counties on Maryland's Eastern Shore had almost an equal number of slaves and freedmen by 1860.[8]

County	Free	Slaves
Kent	3,411	2,509
Queen Anne's	3,372	4,174
Talbot	2,964	3,725
Caroline	2,786	739
Dorchester	4,684	4,123

Worcester	3,571	3,648
Somerset	4,571	5,089
	25,359	24,007

During the Civil War many of these former Marylanders served in Pennsylvania units in various capacities except as armed soldiers. When some Chester Blacks offered to form a military fighting company, authorities turned thumbs-down on the proposal.[9] Ironically, the 87th Pennsylvania Volunteer Regiment, which was to engage in the violent St. Petersburg campaign, had under its command the 39th Regiment, U.S. Colored Troops which was composed of former slaves from Maryland.[10]

During the 1870-80 decade, Delaware County's Black population jumped 90 percent, the great majority residing in Chester. In the aftermath of Emancipation, Delaware migrants now equaled those Pennsylvania-born Blacks in the city. By this period, according to the 1880 U.S. Census, a sizable number of these families resided in the lower Market Street section where the Robert Wade Neighborhood House, a social work establishment, was organized earlier by a Quaker family[11] that freed their slaves in 1711.

Black Community Thrives

Over the subsequent years, the community began thriving with race-owned institutions and enterprises. For example, brothers John and Ellis Watts, and Lorenzo Nugent operated retail stores; Thomas Little was a hotel keeper who had two sons—one a barber, the other an engineer. Charles Fausett was an herb doctor, a practice long popular among rural folks. Other males were listed as white-washers, carters, hucksters, wood-sawyers, coachmen or watermen.[12] (Interestingly, in the mid-1940s, George Nugent, a son of Lorenzo, still operated a grocery store in the same section. He was also rumored to be "the richest colored man in Chester.")

Next to seeking secure livelihoods in a new environment, most Blacks' natural desires are usually to organize for religious activities. The first congregation in Chester, the Union African Methodist Episcopal Church, was founded in 1845 by Robert Morris, an ex-slave.[13] That denomination owned a proud history of fighting slavery, so it was in good company with the Quaker-

Politics and Prejudice

St. Daniel's United Methodist Church is the city's oldest Black congregation occupying its original edifice.

sponsored Neighborhood House. By 1890 there were nine churches of various sizes in the sections where Blacks had spread: Asbury AME (1845), Second and Market Streets; St. Daniel's Methodist Episcopal (1871) in south Chester; St. John's African Union Methodist Protestant (1874), Seventeenth and Walnut Streets[14] were among the earliest. One of the most significant establishments catering to the race, the Funeral Parlor of John and Mary F. Parker, was located at Tenth Street and Edgmont Avenue, approximately halfway between the two predominant Black neighborhoods.

Probably the most famous resident on Yarnell Street, three blocks past Flower, was the future international vaudeville star and songstress, Ethel Waters. Born in 1900 to a 13-year-old mother and a wayward father, she related some of her both comic and tragic experiences in her autobiography, *His Eye Is On The Sparrow*. As a virtual orphan at an early age, one of her numerous guardians was her "aunt" Katie Colder, whom she never failed to visit during her highly successful career. As a sixth grade pupil at Watts Elementary School, Ethel was talked into marrying one Merritt "Buddy" Purnsley, a steel worker more than twice her age.

Chapter 1

Ethel Waters and park named for her.
Waters photo: Library of Congress, Prints
& Photographs Division, Carl Van Vechten
Collection, Lot 12735, no. 1151

So, after getting permission from elders to complete the semester, she undertook her marital responsibilities. But upon learning that her marriage license had been forged by an older woman, she abandoned the false arrangement.[15]

Purnsley, a police department employee in the 1940s, still clung to the notoriety of having been "Ethel Waters's husband." Incidentally, Purnsley's vocations were somewhat typical of the average Black male's job history through the years. Most worked in the lowest level jobs in one of the numerous steel mills or oil refineries. A few of the more fortunate ones secured jobs as municipal custodians or street sweepers, particularly through political henchmen. Females generally were employed as domestics.

Eventually Black residences spread to other parts of the city, a few located in small pockets surrounded by whites. In fact, some of these tiny thoroughfares were without names when the 1880 census was recorded. For instance, one enumerator merely listed the location of several Black-occupied homes as "between Fulton and Penn Street and Second and Third Sts." However, others of these homes were listed as being located in such interesting and curious places as Banana Alley, Irish Alley, Long Bottom Gut,

Froggy Bottom, Liberia Alley and Nugent Court. Many of these names were evidently proffered by residents out of a sense of humor, pride or sarcasm.

But whatever possessed someone to pin the biblical cognomen "Bethel Court" to the lower Market Street section, no one seems to remember. It became the city's "red-light" district situated in the four blocks between the police headquarters and the river docks from where fun-seeking sailors always emerged. Dens of prostitution and other vices flourished undisturbed. The Court's unsavory reputation ultimately began causing the relocation of numerous Black families and establishments, particularly to south Chester, which prior to 1870 had been a separate borough. The main Black-occupied homes in this section were located between Tilghman and Flower Streets, from Norris west to Townsend Street, and on minor thoroughfares between West Third Street and Delaware Avenue. Early on, the entire West Third was dominated by white businesses. The region south of Townsend to the city boundary was the domain of first- and second-generation whites mainly of Eastern European descent.

1910 Business Survey

Black residents, on the other hand, had spread principally to three different sections, progressing steadily in various socioeconomic endeavors. A 1910 survey by the Pennsylvania Negro Business Directory revealed some notable statistics concerning Chester's estimated six thousand minority group residents. Commercial and business establishments included:

Six groceries, two odorless excavators (outhouse cleaners), three public cab companies, six general contractors, three ice and coal merchants, seven dressmakers, two undertakers, eight restaurants, two hotels, two pool halls and three barber shops. T. N. Drew, in fact, owned three eateries, one at Eighth Street and Morton Avenue, another at Second Street and Edgmont Avenue and the third, the Palm Gardens, at Third and Reaney Streets. A unique business was the Chester Industrial School, organized and presided by the Rev. Thomas M. Thomas, a Lincoln University alumnus and founder of the Fifth Presbyterian Church in 1899. Students were trained in dressmaking, millinery, upholstering

Chapter 1

and tailoring, with the finished products being sold publicly to bring in income for supporting the school. Florence Henry also operated a dressmaking shop on the second floor of a building at 608 Central, where her mother, Mrs. W. A. Henry, ran a grocery store on the ground floor.[16]

One Black-owned building surviving over the years was at the corner of Third and Central. It was the Wright Hotel,[17] owned by Emory, a son of Perry A. Wright, a versatile businessman who was born in 1831 in Maryland. The popular hostelry was eventually inherited by a son of Emory, E. Courtlandt. Later, a patent medicine shop was operated on the building's street floor, and finally a tavern.

Professionals in that period included public schoolteachers, two physicians, numerous ministers and an attorney, W. H. Ridley of Media, but who also had an office in south Chester. In political, public positions were two Blacks on the school board, and two serving on the city council, Will Mack and Arthur Reed.

As in the cases of other burgeoning Black communities across the nation, this city also had its share of secret fraternal orders. These institutions were presumed to instill in their members' spiritual strength of purpose as well as social satisfaction in themselves

Chester Industrial School.

and their communities. Moreover, these movements appealed to their philosophical, emotional and religious nature. Such secret orders indeed predated Black churches in some sections of the country during pre-Emancipation years when social or religious gatherings of Blacks were forbidden, sometimes under the pain of death.

In the first decade of the new twentieth century, Black lodges in town included two Grand Orders of Odd Fellows, five Knights of Pythias, three Tent Sisters, a Masonic, a Grand United Order of True Believers and a Women's Christian Temperance Union. John A. Watts, for whom a Pythias lodge was named, would later be afforded the same honor by the newly organized Improved Benevolent and Protective Order of Elks of the World.[18] Most of these associations dressed proudly in their distinctive, colorful attire during holiday parades or special religious services. Most, especially the Elks, established annual scholarship funds for deserving and needy students.

Only a handful of Black parents in this town were financially capable of sending their high school graduating son or daughter off to an institution of higher learning. And those students aspiring to seek the teaching profession could—and often did—matriculate at such nearby colleges as Lincoln University or Cheyney Training School for Teachers, both located no more than 30 miles in either direction from their homes. Both institutions were sponsored by liberal white groups—Cheyney by Quakers and Lincoln by Presbyterians—yet returning teachers were invariably subjected to being victims of discrimination foisted upon them by their own race—their political leaders in particular.

Though there were no local or state segregation laws pertaining to education, nonetheless these teachers were assigned to jim-crow facilities, a situation approved by the school board at the behest of a few so-called leaders. There evidently existed among some a notion that their college-trained sons and daughters were incapable of competing successfully against white applicants in certification examinations.

Around 1910, there were only sixteen instructors needed for the four small segregated schools.[19] As the Black population increased, additional qualified teachers, who happened to be outside the political circle, had a price to pay for the desired appointment. It became almost common knowledge that certain political henchmen had to have their "palms greased" before giving the go-ahead for a teaching post for a Black. At that period of time, it may not actually have been so difficult for some unsuspecting souls to understand that a few hard-working parents who scrounged funds in order to send a son or daughter to college would later agree to make a "contribution"—monetary or otherwise—for that prestigious position.

Such shady manipulations doubtlessly were laying the work for a future political machine, fueled by some race leaders, that ultimately would run roughshod over legal rights of virtually every aspect in the lives of the Black residents in particular. And by obligingly easing the path of the dominant bandwagon, it seemed that most of these taxpaying citizens were embracing the philosophy of racial subordination as espoused by Booker T. Washington, generally accepted nationwide as the leader of his race. To a certain degree, it may have been more appropriate had these pillars of the community adopted the uncompromising, indomitable spirit of the likes of Frederick Douglass, Harriett Tubman, Henry H. Garnett, Samuel Cornish or Daniel Coker, those true "freedom fighters" whose roots were nurtured in the soil of Maryland, the birthplace of many of the town's Black populace. Of course, if their forebears were not aware of these giant crusaders, decades certainly would pass before their offspring would discover them in their school history books.

Yet, to the credit of some gentlemen who kowtowed to political expediency, they would soon be afforded the opportunities to demonstrate their courage and true convictions by risking life and limb to protect their loved ones. Some went overseas in World War I to make their city and country "safe for democracy," while others simultaneously risked the same protecting their families against white mobs during the 1917 race riots in Chester.

Summer of 1917 Riot in Chester

As war raged in Europe, racial tensions in Chester increased among Blacks and whites, especially newly arriving southerners

Politics and Prejudice

and those of foreign extraction. Many of the latter groups were unskilled, consequently fomenting bitter competition with Blacks for jobs in the numerous steel and chemical foundries now on wartime production schedules. Having had a virtual monopoly on the unskilled and low-paying jobs, many were in positions to recommend friends or relatives when additional help was being recruited. Unfortunately for the foreign-born, many of whom had a language problem, white Americans did not always welcome them as residents to their neighborhoods. So, as not a few of these foreigners tended to look unjustifiably upon Blacks as scapegoats for their predicaments, this sentiment invariably mixed with the southerners' traditional anti-Black perception. The city was extremely ripe for racial conflagration.

Wild Scenes of Disorder Checked by the Police

Forty-Eight Injured Persons Treated at the Chester Hospital and at the City Hall, while Many Others Were Cared for at Home— Police Surgeon on Duty the Greater Part of the Night.

GRAPHIC DETAILS OF A NIGHT OF TERROR IN THE CITY

Headlines in July 26, 1917 edition of *Chester Times*.

Chester, like scores of American cities, became victim of racial mayhem and murder during the summer of 1917. Trouble first exploded here on July 25 with the killing of a white man by a Black during an argument of unknown cause.[20] For several days mobs of both races fought running battles with guns, knives and clubs. Much of the war zone was along West Third Street.

24

In one incident, a mob of approximately three hundred whites was chasing a lone Black, who suddenly turned, drew a pistol and fired several shots into the mob, killing one of his pursuers. The Black was then chased into a house near Third and Lloyd. The mob set fire to the building. Soon, fortunately, a posse under the leadership of Mayor McDowell arrived in time to disperse the angry mob and rescue the would-be victim.[21]

At another time during the riots, a horde dragged two Blacks from a trolley car, shooting one fatally through the head; the second intended victim escaped. The two men had been seen conversing with a white man on the trolley. Another innocent victim, Policeman James Jarrett, was shot to death while trying to control another outbreak.[22] Fortunately for both sides of the conflict, the "uncontrollable" mobs wisely adopted enough self-control not to venture into the predominantly Black neighborhoods, just a few blocks from their own battle sectors. After nearly a week of rioting and at least a half-dozen deaths and hundreds of injuries, the violence was brought to an end by city policemen, aided by state troopers.[23] Mayor William McDowell, in contrast to the outright negligence or vacillation shown by some authorities in other cities during this troubled summer, displayed forthright courage and impartial action in handling the riots. Obviously always having enjoyed fair relations with Blacks, McDowell operated a haberdashery on West Third Street near Reaney for many years.

The name of an unlikely ally of the besieged minority group, interestingly enough, has surfaced years afterwards. Whether a public relations ploy or not, during that period and down through the years there has spread scuttlebutt that young John J. McClure, son of a county political operative, had arranged to secure firearms for the embattled Blacks.[24] McClure, a former Swarthmore College student, became county GOP boss soon afterwards.

The genesis of the persistent rumor is difficult to pin down, yet it becomes more credible in view of his later involvement in seamy public incidents.

Almost simultaneous to the riots, new organizations were being formed for civic betterment and progress of the Black race, including the Ruth L. Bennett Home for Negro Girls and the John

Politics and Prejudice

Ruth L. Bennett Home and Wilson Nursery were two of the important community agencies not affected by Commodore Barry Bridge later crossing the city.

A. Watts Elks Lodge, to cite two for their longevity.

Mrs. Bennett, founder of the establishment, a graduate of Storer College, arrived in town in 1914 with her husband, the Rev. J. R. Bennett, new pastor of the Calvary Baptist Church. Her overriding concern was the need of homes and hospitality for the scores of young women migrating from the south, noting that the city jail was the only place they could sleep for one night at a time. By 1917, she opened the Home for Negro Girls in a spacious residential building at Second Street and Reaney. Her husband shortly afterwards founded the Providence Baptist Church, yet continued friendly relations with Calvary Church. By 1928, Mrs. Bennett established the city's first day care center for Black children, naming it the William Wilson Nursery in honor of the donor, a white businessman. The original all-female board of directors was joined by males in 1943.

John A. Watts, a prominent citizen, left his mark on the Black community in the fields of education, politics and religion, also. The Elks Lodge bearing his name was organized in 1917 in a building located at Second Street and Edgmont Avenue, one of the early Black neighborhoods. As Exalted Ruler, his leadership was largely responsible for the swift growth in membership resulting in the construction of larger headquarters on West Second Street, a few doors from the Ruth L. Bennett Home. The Watts Elementary School was named in his honor; and in 1884, he led a committee to procure land for the erection of the original brick structure for St. Daniel's Methodist Church, located a half block from Watts School. Over the years the lodge hall has served as a community facility for meetings, concerts and bazaars, and during the period of Pennsylvania's "Blue Laws" offered Sunday entertainment for members and their friends. In keeping with the policies of the national Grand Lodge, the local affiliate sponsored educational scholarships for local graduating students. Its Exalted Rulers have included politically connected individuals such as Lewis M. Hunt, Albert A. Reading and E. Courtlandt Wright, to name a few.

SOME CAME SOONER THAN WILLIAM PENN
Bibliography

1. Samuel T. Wiley, *Cyclopedia of Delaware County, Pa.* (New York: Gresham Publishers, 1894), pp. 108-9.

2. Ibid.

3. Jeffrey R. Brackett, *The Negro in Maryland* (Baltimore: Johns Hopkins University, 1899), p. 85.

4. Ibid, p. 108. A Maryland law of 1831 ruled "It is not lawful for any free negro or negroes, slave or slaves to assemble or attend any meeting for religious purposes unless conducted by a white licensed or ordained preachers or some reputable white person or persons of the neighborhood. . . ." ch. 323 s 7.

5. Brackett, *The Negro in Maryland*, pp. 97, 111.

6. Charles L. Blockson, *The Underground Railroad in Pennsylvania* (Jacksonville, N.C.: Flame International, 1981), p. 63.

7. Ibid, p. 64.

8. U.S. Census, 1860.

9. Wiley, *Cyclopedia*, p. 77.

10. National Archives. U.S. Colored Troops.

11. Wiley, *Cyclopedia*, p. 108.

12. U.S. Census, City of Chester, 1900.

13. Wiley, *Cyclopedia*, pp. 99, 120-21.

14. Ibid, p. 169.

15. Ethel Waters with Charles Samuels, *His Eye Is On the Sparrow* (New York: Alfred Knopf, 1951), autobiography of Ethel Waters' early life in Chester.

16. J. H. W. Howard, *Pennsylvania Negro Business Directory* (Harrisburg, 1909), p. 91.

17. Ibid, pp. 92-3.

18. Ibid, pp. 94-96.

19. Ibid. p. 95.

20. *New York Times*, July 26, 1917; also *Chester Times*.

21. Ibid, July 27, 1917; *Chester Times*.

22. Ibid, July 28, 1917; *Chester Times* reported shot in ankle; *New York Times* said he was killed.

23. Ibid, July 29, 1917; *Chester Times*.

24. Francis D. Tyson, *Negro Migration, 1916-17* (U.S. Dept. of Labor, 1919), pp. 131-33. The writer in the chapter "Friction in the North" claimed to throw additional light on the riots. "The trouble probably took its rise from friction between the worst of both groups," he wrote. "Trouble had been brewing at a notorious saloon in Bethel Court being run by a political henchman."

Chapter 2

Political Machine Gears Up (1910-25)

JOHN McCLURE PICKS BLACK BOSSES; RACE RIOTS EXPLODE

The political entanglements of the Black population that caught them unaware began when their leaders of the 1930-40 decade were mere lads in knee-pants and their sisters were playing hopscotch. Someone once jokingly referred to Chester as "McClure's Plantation." But truthfully, it seemed closer to an early-century "company town," wherein the all-powerful proprietor and his straw-bosses held sway over many phases of community doings, both through his designs and the inhabitants' willingness to allow the system to continue unchallenged. The supreme boss in question was John J. McClure.

This 21-year-old Swarthmore College dropout took over control of the Delaware County Republican organization from his father in 1917. He then proceeded to fashion one of the "most solid political machines in modern American history," according to one source. He was often compared to other notorious political bosses who ruled over their particular bailiwicks through cronyism or iron fists—the likes of Ed Crump of Memphis, Frank Hague of Jersey City, Tom Pendergast of Kansas City or James Curley of Boston. Interestingly, the latter two gentlemen spent time in prison for their illicit doings, yet John McClure never spent a night in the hoosegow, even though courts had found him guilty of betraying public trust on two distinct, widespread occasions.

Crusading newspapers in their particular domains were often instrumental in exposing nefarious activities of certain political operatives. Not so with the local daily *Chester Times*, flourishing since 1871. For a long time, the editors used kid gloves and tap-danced softly around the questionable performances of the slick ringmaster. Seldom was he featured in an unfavorable light; few can recall seeing his photo in the newspapers.

A tall, thin, balding man during the early 1940s, he might have served as a perfect model for the farmer-preacher in Wood's

Politics and Prejudice

BOSS — John J. McClure.
Courtesy of Delaware County Historical
Society, Pennsylvania

"Gothic American" painting, except that McClure's control was more lucrative and expansive, his handymen more docile. "John McClure made me, and he can break me." Such a statement uttered by a nervous appointee doubtlessly represented the sentiment of countless other recipients of political favors.

First elected to the Pennsylvania State Senate in 1928, he was convicted three years later on charges of rum-running in Chester.[1] Fortunately for him, McClure escaped an eighteen-month prison term and $50,000 fine due to repeal of the Eighteenth Amendment of the United States Constitution. Soon afterwards, he shrewdly gained control of the Delaware County supervisors and committee chairmen, thereby creating his own self-styled "War Board" to solidify his position. Soon, the "man on the eighth floor" of the Crozer Building, the city's tallest structure, kept a careful eye on virtually every facet of the Black community— schools, housing, law enforcement, recreation, plus certain jobs in industry. Moreover, if anything escaped his view, there were certain underlings to report to him.

An astute old-timer who never kowtowed to the machine offered one explanation as to how the faction manipulated to assure control over certain residential groups. "McClure's chief man in the Ninth Ward was Ed Fry," he recalled. "Fry always saw to it that Black families in need of fuel or food were taken care of.

Or if your son was arrested by police, he would arrange to get him off, providing the case wasn't too serious." Continuing, he added, "Sometimes he would recommend a lawyer, for free. And he could get your father a street-sweeper or janitor job. So, on election day, who're gonna vote for?" McClure, who sometimes had a shaky alliance with the powerful industrialist Pew clan, was known to send prospective employees to their Sun Shipyard or Sun Oil plant, both of which hired Blacks only as laborers.

White Tavern Owner Runs Ninth Ward

Ed Fry, the white overall boss in the Black-dominated Ninth Ward, operated a hotel-tavern on the corner of the Seventh Street and Central Avenue intersection where Booker T. Washington and Frederick Douglass school buildings eventually occupied two other corners. Thus, to some residents during those early lean days, it may have seemed a fair trade-off for some of the earnings from Fry's liquor sales to be offered back to poor households as ultimate political leverage. While other towns or neighborhoods would often successfully protest the close proximity of liquor-dispensing establishments to their schools, Fry's business nonetheless operated for decades, despite the spectacle of fights and other examples disorderliness occurring during school hours. The so-called legal argument in Fry's favor was that the tavern had existed in that location long before the schools were constructed. Yet, when a portion of the federal housing project had originally been scheduled to include the tavern site, obvious political persuasion caused cancellation of the plan. The Fry tavern was to remain in place for decades longer.

Although residing in a precinct miles away, Fry also kept a hand in the selection of Black teachers, along with Lewis M. Hunt, during the latter's tenure as the lone Black on the Chester School Board. The tavern owner was also known to have brokered marriages of convenience among relatives of the Black political leaders, presumably in attempts to strengthen a minority hierarchy that, according to a 1945 finding, showed that at least twenty of the total fifty-seven Black teachers were relatives or close associates of the community's political clique.[2]

There appeared, furthermore, some instances of cruel restrictions

Politics and Prejudice

Lewis M. Hunt and his funeral home.

being foisted upon some professionals wanting to pursue the normal life of caring citizens. For decades there existed an unsubstantiated edict in the community that no female teacher could be hired unless she was single. As a consequence, there were generally known several examples of secret marriages wherein female teachers and their spouses had to live apart. One of the better-known cases was that of a popular professional couple living for years under such an arrangement, who had to allow their offspring to be raised in another city by relatives.

The primary Black lieutenants in the McClure order holding sway between the 1930s and 1950s included Casper H. Green, Lewis M. Hunt, Albert A. Reading, Edgar Richardson and E. Courtlandt Wright.

Probably the most visible and consequently accessible to his constituents was Green, the Black alderman in the Ninth Ward. His West Third Street office was generally the hangout of his political cronies, yet he always made himself available to discuss any problems with other citizens. He would make no bones concerning his relations with the GOP organization, citing his consistent elections to his post. He could anticipate no change in community conditions "until you folks are willing to work hard for reforms," he once told a group of young would-be reformers in the privacy of his office. The son of an early Marylander, Jeremiah Green, Sr., an insurance man and assistant Murphy AME Church pastor, Alderman Green's family members teaching in the public

Chapter 2

From left: Caspar H. Green, Albert H. Reading, E. Courtlandt Wright.

school system included a sister, Leanne; a sister-in-law Bertha Green, and her daughter, Millicent.

Lewis M. Hunt, a Georgia-born mulatto who could easily pass for white, served several terms on the Chester School Board of Education, having been elected in city-wide voting, along with other white members. He was the most successful mortician among city Blacks, and thus presumably not necessarily dependent upon political favoritism for his family's livelihood. At one period he caused the school board and its superintendent to order the elimination of pages in a citywide textbook giving derogatory descriptions of American Blacks. He, too, often strongly urged citizens to bring their complaints to school board sessions. For the lack of credible representative organizations, other than the old-line professionals-dominated NAACP, such advice went unheeded until the mid- 1940s. Almost all Black teachers' appointments came through at least the tacit approval of Hunt, and it had been long rumored that female prospects in particular were obligated to pay a "fee" in some form or another to the carpetbagger Fry.

Hunt suddenly resigned his school board seat in 1944 for "domestic reasons." According to a story in the daily Chester Times concerning the matter, he had been involved in an assault incident with a young teacher. Rumors spread that McClure had forced Hunt's resignation on account the negative publicity spawned by the incident. If that were actually true, then the man twice convicted of crimes[3] obviously held a double standard for one of his Black officeholders. Nonetheless, no discernible objections were heard among Blacks concerning the ouster of Hunt, who continued active in civic affairs. The Rev. Daniel A. Scott, pastor of Bethany Baptist Church, was appointed as Hunt's successor.

"Bert" Reading, also son of an early family, was a flamboyant character who served alternately as a county deputy sheriff or a chauffeur. The switches in his jobs were dependent either on budget or disciplinary matters, as decided by his immediate supervisors at the County Courthouse in Media. Personally, at least, he could claim an unusual kinship with boss-man McClure, for Reading, a defendant in the rum-running case, had been given an eighteen-month sentence and a year probation for his role in the crime.[4] Never a resident of any predominant Black ward or precinct, nonetheless the bombastic Reading quite often was called upon to participate as master of ceremonies at church or civic events. Very few holiday parades, in fact, occurred sans Bert as the strutting majordomo. He held such prominent positions as Exalted Ruler of the Elks Lodge and commander of the Charles Horsey Post of the American Legion. Perennially driving a black Cadillac sedan, regardless of his current station, he apparently savored his role as a GOP point-man among blacks, often dispensing rumors he claimed were "straight from the horse's mouth." An example of his tactic was his reportedly spreading misleading information that tenants of the first proposed federal housing project, initially opposed by the GOP faction, would be forced to turn off electricity at 9:00 P.M. The Reading family, otherwise, was of solid stock. Samuel Reading, Sr. had been one of the earliest Chester policemen; two sons, Samuel, Jr. and Lester, owned well-known printing businesses.

Though not elected to any position higher than precinct committeeman, Edgar "Nuts" Richardson, who earned a reputation in his adolescent days as a flashy sandlot baseball player, seldom became involved in any civic or political tug-of-war. The always immaculately-attired gentleman, however, enjoyed clout enough to see to it that his two sons secured positions in the law enforcement sector. The eldest, Jack, served as a constable in Alderman Green's office. The other son, Leroy,

Chapter 2

was a city policeman. Despite his personal relations with the law enforcement elements, hearsay existed that the elder Richardson earned part of his upkeep as a moneylender. In a surprising, presumed political union, Jack Richardson and Millicent Green, a niece of Casper Green, were married in the prime of their respective careers. Here, incidentally, was an example giving lie to the long-held understanding that barred married female teachers from holding jobs in the school system. The inside report was that the aging Ed Fry helped arrange the union because he was interested in grooming bachelor Jack to succeed him as a powerful Ninth Ward boss.

"Court" Wright, long considered an important and respected cog in the Black section of the machine, always seemingly played his hands close to the vest. His grandfather was Perry A. Wright,[5] born during slavery, who later made a small fortune as a businessman. As a community leader, an elementary school was named in his honor. Court Wright first operated a patent medicine store and later a well-operated tavern patronized primarily by professional males. He and his wife, Anne, founder of the "25 Club" that was involved in charitable causes, became active in the St. Mary's Episcopal Church. Most of the time Wright managed his own businesses yet for some unknown reasons, he worked briefly during World War II as a state Liquor Store clerk, a job requiring no particular political pull. Later, he was appointed as a detective in the Delaware County offices. Finally, he served with the Housing Authority. Meanwhile, his son, Robert, was finishing college and would serve in the Army, later to attend law school. If it seemed that for some reason "Court" had been bounced around the political arena, the Wright family would ultimately enjoy the most prestigious prizes of all.

Had the Richardson-Green nuptial partnership endured (which it did not), an offspring might have led to the succession of the local Black political oligarchy. Through the past years, numerous political lieutenants inherited their mantles through their forebears, including the elder Richardson whose father, J. Allen, was a school custodian; or Bert Reading, whose father, Samuel, Sr., was a policeman. Later came certain professionals who quickly formed alliance with the clique, capitalizing on their presumed

Politics and Prejudice

popularity with the rank and file. Lewis M. Hunt and several latecomers would fit in this category.

For the most part these leaders, who unswervingly did the biddings of their boss, received no earthly reward, save earnings from their specific vocations. Most, moreover, spent their entire lives in their original Eighth or Ninth Ward homes—which often paled in comparison with abodes later constructed by other middle-class families. Reading, the only politico not residing in the predominantly Black districts, still occupied the home where his family lived in 1900.

While most of these gentlemen were unable—for financial as well as loyalty reasons—to move from their birthplaces, John McClure, who escaped prison after his rum-running conviction, was at it again. In 1943, he was indicted for conspiring to sell the Chester Water Company to a private syndicate. Fortunately, he and four City Councilmen were acquitted but ordered to return to the city coffers the $250,000 profits they hoped to pocket.

Operators of existing freewheeling gambling joints and policy rackets*, on the other hand, siphoned off some of their profits to some authorities in higher places. True, such operators were sometimes victims of ersatz raids by police, so ordered because of suspected welshing on expected payoffs, or it being near election time. Such raids might lull residents into believing reform efforts from the city were soon due.

In contrast, there were penalties aimed at otherwise loyal Black leaders suspected of straying from the straight-and-narrow path as determined by the GOP chiefs. Bert Reading's elevator moves, from deputy sheriff to chauffeur and back, were among the more notable examples of these tactics. Court Wright's harmless patent medicine store was once subjected to a police raid, more or less obviously to humiliate the family always involved in church or charitable activities. Also, there was Hunt's forced resignation from the school board in wake of his alleged incident with a

---

*"Policy rackets" were illegal lotteries. If you wanted to place a bet without leaving your home or office, you could arrange for a "numbers runner" to come by to accept your money.

young woman.

All the while, much more serious illegal and immoral paradoxical events were thriving, including houses of prostitution operating full blast for years in the small thoroughfare of Bethel Court, the so-called "red-light" district, located less than four city blocks from the Police headquarters.

Black Democrats Heartened Briefly

Whatever criticism they heard of their cavalier attitude towards the city and county populace, the intransigent powers-that-be faced only two electoral challenges during the 1936-46 decade. On each occasion, Black GOP leaders were sure to keep their constituents in line. When George Earle became the third Democrat since the Civil War to be elected as the state governor, there were faint, encouraging rumblings among young Chester Blacks idling their times away in pool halls and street corners, complaining about local problems, the lack of progressive leadership and economic opportunities.

Catching their attention soon were placards beginning to be plastered on vacant buildings and telephone poles. The messages, proclaimed in bold red letters, said: TELL THEM WE ARE RISING. Listed below were names of several Philadelphia Blacks appointed to important positions by Governor Earle, including Joseph H. Rainey as state Athletic Commissioner and J. Austin Norris as deputy attorney general. Other Democrats elected to the State Legislature included the first woman, Crystal Bird Fauset; Hobson R. Reynolds, author of the first state Equal Rights Bill; and the Rev. Marshal Shepherd, who had spoken to Chester audiences several times in the past.

Such a concise source of news pertaining to their race, unfortunately, could not offer any comprehensive details on the manner in which such progressive accomplishments could come about. And to make matters worse, the young ambitious Blacks were in a community where radios were considered a luxury, and where the daily paper seldom elaborated on news of positive accomplishments among Blacks, wherever their residencies.

All so briefly, those neglected groups entertained some hope of becoming allied with some faction whose leadership might be capable of offering some competition to local Black representatives of the machine. A handful of Blacks willing to identify themselves publicly as Democrats included Sherman Williams, a U.S. Postal Service employee; Oliver Turpin, a contractor; William Willis, a store owner; and Richard Thomas, a Morgan College and Wharton School of Finance graduate. Incredibly enough, the best the state Democratic administration could offer Thomas was a job as interviewer in the Chester branch of the state Employment office. These were the days of the WPA (Works Progress Administration), NYA (National Youth Administration) and similar New Deal programs conducted largely in recreation centers or evening school classrooms. These projects did provide employment for numerous college-training Blacks unable to receive job considerations through the local GOP. Although McClure lost his statewide influence during the Roosevelt sweep in 1936, he nonetheless was destined to retain exclusive control over Delaware County and Chester for many years to come.

POLITICAL MACHINE GEARS UP
Bibliography

1. *New York Times*, November 7, November 24, 1933. Reading was one of the numerous McClure associates handed suspended sentences in the rum-running conspiracy.

2. R. E. Harris, *Delinquency In Our Democracy* (Philadelphia: Wetzel Publishing, 1954), p. 25.

3. *New York Times*, April 30, 1943.

4. J. H. W. Howard & Son, *Pennsylvania Negro Business Directory* (Harrisburg, Pa., 1910), p. 96.

Chapter 3

South Chester, A Thriving Community (1926-35)

BUSINESSES, ENTERTAINMENT RAISE PRIDE; NAACP CONSERVATIVES OUSTED

Had young strangers come to south Chester's Black community in the 1930s, they probably would have thought "all is well" despite the city's overall segregation practices. Black-owned businesses operated primarily along Central Avenue and West Third Street. Schools were orderly, presided over by such highly respected pedagogues as W. K. Valentine, principal of Booker T. Washington Junior High; or Carrie M. Pipes, principal of Watts Elementary. Most instructors held degrees from either Cheyney State, West Chester Teachers, Morgan College or Lincoln University of Oxford, Pennsylvania. Booker T. had its Maroon and Gray football squad coached by James H. Grasty, a Lincoln ex-grid captain, who also taught academic classes.

During spring months semi-pro basketball games were staged at the Benn Theater on Central, featuring the home team, the "Jack Morris Five," an aggregation owned by its namesake who was reputedly the illegitimate son of former Pennsylvania Governor Sproul. Its players included such favorites as "Red" Moore, "Slats" Davis, Lonnie Shields and "Happy" Handy, the latter sometimes doubling as the high-stepping majordomo during the Elks parade. At other times the building management sponsored amateur shows or boxing matches that often highlighted duels featuring pugilists with such nom de plumes as "Kid Kanky," "Cool Breeze" or "Popper Stopper."

The multi-purpose building, later re-christened the "Roxie Theater," began showing all-Black movies, many of which presented a sociological or historical plot. Wherein the assigned school textbooks offered only a limited knowledge of Black history-makers, these movies could have the power to transport young minds far off into a Black fantasyland full of larger-than-life heroes whom they could hope to emulate sometime in the future. An example was the great actor Paul Robeson, their best-known versatile idol whose real-life career could be matched by only a very few whites—All-American football player, lawyer, opera star, concert singer and a crusader for democracy.

Moreover, there flashed across the silver screen other sepia stars that producers tended to equate with white performers. Nina Mae McKinney, for instance, was dubbed the "Black Garbo"; Lorenzo Tucker, the "Black Valentino"; Bea Freeman, the "Sepia Mae West" and Ethel Moses, the "Harlem Harlow." Black cowboys portrayed by the likes of suave Ralph Cooper were often viewed as reverse emulation of whites; the young viewers clearly not yet realizing that Black cowboys performed vital roles in the making of the American West.

Autumn Sunday afternoons were the times football fans converged at the old Fairgrounds, a former horse racetrack in Chester Township, just across the city boundary line. The Comets A.C., a local semi-pro team, was organized and coached by Stan Jackson, a one-time Temple University player. Starting in 1926, the squad's eight-year history boasted of a record of 63 wins and 6 losses. Frankly, the nicknames of most of the squad members might have given pause to visiting opponents hoping for an equal chance of victory.

Believe it or not, some of the players answered to these names even in everyday life—Mutt Coleman, Ham Brown, Neck Stanley, Scrap Black, Feet White, Doggie Roseboro, Piggy Hunt, Skip Purnsley, Bones Taylor, Gatemouth Fontaine, Yum-Yum Perrigan, Fat Morris,

Stan Jackson's Comets: won 63, lost 6, tied 2.

Taddy Lock, Biggy Bell and Babe Harris. The Comets and their followers particularly looked forward to the annual contests with two local white teams wherein either side evidently considered it a matter of ethnic pride to come off the field victorious. Those foes were the Lloyd Street A.C., composed of predominantly Irish bullies, and the St. Hedwigs A.C., whose squad was made up of Polish men. The two clubs' headquarters were at either ends of the Black community, and no welcome mats were ever spread for Blacks walking through their enclaves. The Comet fans minus any grandstands, however, never tried to reciprocate any hostilities towards these two visiting aggregations or their followers.

The brains behind the Comets' operation was Solomon "Alex" Bouldin, the popular barber who also trained young boxers, including Jimmy Moore, Charley Burley and Ike Trimble, who became fairly successful club fighters. Besides utilizing the gym at St. Hedwig's Catholic Church to train his young charges, Alex also enjoyed a long working relationship with Jimmy Dougherty, the "Baron of Leiperville," whose best-known protege was heavyweight George Godfrey. A young Sugar Ray Robinson also trained at Dougherty's quarters when in the area.

West Third Street Main Drag

Approximately seven blocks along West Third Street was considered the "main drag" for most of the Black residents, including those coming from sections miles away. Especially on weekdays, they came to the barber shops, beauty salons, restaurants, private social clubs, beer gardens, pool parlors, or Miller's Pharmacy, all race-owned. This was the thoroughfare where friends and acquaintances met and hung out, joking or ruminating on current race issues. Many of the young elements, chiefly high school or college students, often met outside Miller's Drug Store, ogling the passing crowds during the evenings; "drug store cowboys," they were dubbed....

> "Here comes my Black friend," one youth whispers to his pal, quickly adding, "he don't mind me calling him that. He's my boon-coon."

> "Man, he's got his hair conked and all shining ... And that pig-meat he's got on his arm, she's 38 and 2, forty with me," the other quipped.
>
> "Yeah, but her other old man, he was a tusk-hog. He'd want to cut you a brand new one if you tried to make her." "Well, we better move on because Doc Miller's afraid we might break his windows, standing so close to them."
>
> "Say, Joe, let's truck on down to the Central Avenue block party and watch the Charleston contest. Wanna bet whose team wins—Jazz Hunt or Bob Colder?"

Other businesses, owned by whites, included fruit and seafood stands and grocery stores. At the west end of the street's Black section sat the Strand movie house, owned by Mathew "Mack" Margoline, a Jewish realtor who designated the upstairs seating for Blacks. Mack, who also rented homes to scores of Blacks, forced them to occupy the last five rows of his ground-floor Apollo Theater at Third and Lloyd Streets. Halfway between the locations of these two jim-crow enterprises was the Morris Mailman haberdashery, which profited exclusively from Black customers for twenty-five years, yet never employed any of their race.

Approximately all other shopping by Blacks was carried on in the city's primary business district on Edgmont Avenue or Market Street—the location of department stores, clothiers, five-and-dime shops and similar establishments. These proprietors obviously had set a hiring policy that was religiously followed by whites in south Chester. However, there appeared to be one slight difference insofar as movie houses were concerned—a few hired Black janitors and permitted their balconies to be optional to white patrons but mandatory to Blacks.

Nearly every young person leaving town to accept a successful position not available in Chester invariably visited Bouldin's Barber Shop during return visits. Always posted on his shop window or on the indoor walls were items or pictures of a local person making noteworthy accomplishments. Interestingly, many young folks, especially those with music or dance ambitions, seemed to prefer high-tailing it off to the "Big Apple" in search of fame or fortune, although Philadelphia, then the nation's third largest city, was a potential mecca for entertainers.

Both the cultural attainments and relative civic progress in the "City of Brotherly Love" were either unknown or unnoticed by the seemingly ambitious. Though still bothered by racial problems which were consistently challenged, that metropolis might have served as a civic role model for Chester's aspiring leaders. The average Black Chesterite indeed had a very limited knowledge of events occurring in the outer world, except for small bits of news gained through weekly Black newspapers available at a few newsstands in their community. And by the same token, out-of-town readers of the *Afro-American*, *Pittsburgh Courier* or the *Philadelphia Tribune* newspapers seldom read of any events transpiring among their brethren in Chester. Even the local daily *Chester Times* generally ignored publishing any news of consequence involving its racial minorities. Suspects in crime stories, however, always were identified by race—that is, for instance, "John Jones, 23, negro. . . . "

For years, some enlightened Blacks expressed hopes of having a young crusading reporter on their side, someone to tell their side of the story and take to task those blocking progress of their race. The few Black students entering Chester High School in the late 1920s could not help but notice the photo of a relay track team that included one of their race. That was Theodore W. Graham, who earlier had earned a track scholarship to Syracuse University. First, to his credit, Graham was one of the few college graduates to return to his home town, bringing with him a degree in journalism. He obtained employment at the local *Times*, yet the only assignment allowed him was writing a column titled "Among Our Colored Citizens." His duties were to collect and write items on social and church activities. Whether he was ever permitted to perform journalistic undertakings commensurate with his training, no such evidence was ever illustrated. Graham left town eventually, serving separate stints with Black papers in Philadelphia, Baltimore and Pittsburgh. His successor for the next three and a half years did extract from the publisher permission to write on civic issues, though he had no formal journalistic training whatsoever.

Conservative NAACP Leaders Ousted

The local NAACP chapter, for a long time until the late 1930s, functioned under the strong influence of a coterie of schoolteachers and clergy persons, many of the former group generally beholden to the political machine for their own welfare. Thus the organization favored a low-key, conservative approach to civil rights matters. Their members, on the other hand, could not become involved in intraracial controversies, particularly in keeping with the association's national policy. An unusual dilemma thus faced the Black community, especially from the younger grass-roots leadership now beginning to assert itself. This latter group gradually moved into the NAACP membership, bent on pursuing a more progressive agenda, much to the embarrassment of the status quo professionals who gradually dropped to the wayside. The newcomers eventually elected as their president Herman Laws, an articulate young man recently out of college. Trained as a teacher, Laws quite understandably had no assignment in the school system, yet worked in the WPA and NYA projects and youth programs.

"Too often," he once remarked, "we have to climb over the backs of our own people to reach the main enemy on our march for racial advancement." As a consequence, some of the top echelon of the revitalized NAACP were forced to wear two hats, organizing the Independent Civic League to tackle problems created by various "Old Guard" political leaders.

For his dubious reward for pioneering a grass-roots awakening, Laws unfortunately was drafted into the military, a fate many of his followers considered politically inspired. His successor as NAACP president would be George T. Raymond who would hold the post for more than two decades. Though far from being as articulate as Laws, Raymond, whom his close friends nicknamed a "bull-headed Marylander," was a diminutive individual who often took on the power brokers single-handedly. A lifelong resident, in his early thirties Raymond also would eventually

Chapter 3

have to fight bigoted dangers threatening his entire family.

Professionals Not Too Clannish

Chester's Black professionals were not as clannish as middle-class folks are sometimes ordinarily pictured by those in the lower socioeconomic category. Moreover, those relatively few physicians, dentists, and numerous schoolteachers who earned their daily bread through regular association with the hoi polloi, most resided in close proximity, even next door to each other. On Flower Street between Third and Fifth Streets, for example, one could note the homes of the Valentines, Brown-Wilsons, Phillips, Harmons, Kellys, Links, Fontaines, Smiths, Bryants, Griffins and Robersons. And on Third Street between Tilghman and Norris at various times the residents were the Moores, Hunts, Ravens, Brodies, Hardys, Henderson and two Thomas families. Many of their social activities were shared with their equals residing in Media, Yeadon, Darby and other suburban towns.

This not to detract anything from the community endeavors of especially the professional women, as many demonstrated a genuine interest in the welfare of young folks. Some were members of the "25 Club" and engaged in charitable work under their president Mrs. E. Courtlandt Wright. Others volunteered their hours raising funds for the underprivileged children of Camp Hope, and still others served with Girl Scout Troops sponsored by either Bethany Baptist or the Fifth Presbyterian churches. Evola Thomas, daughter of a late physician, who was engaged by the local YWCA as its colored works secretary, also enjoyed the support of such women.

Occasionally some of these professional families were struck by tragedy or scandal that might have been hardly noticeable had it occurred to an average Black family. Such incidents could have conceivably denied the community of leadership for which the victims had shown some potential.

Lewis M. Hunt, Jr., son and male heir of his family undertaking business, was mysteriously murdered in New York where he went to reside after graduation from Lincoln University. His sister, Gladys, married the Rev. Milton Galamison who took her to New York where he became a leader in school reform. Perhaps he would have been considered ungrateful to campaign against a segregated school system which his father-in-law helped perpetuate.

Elise Thomas, next-door neighbor to the Hunts, also was killed in New York where she migrated after finishing at Fiske University. She was the sister of Evola Thomas.

J. Hume Miller, son of Dr. T. M. Miller and grandson of the South Carolina Reconstruction congressman Thomas E. Miller, spent his earlier years in a private boarding school, returning to become immensely popular with his age-group. Upon completion of his college education and training as a funeral director, he married and opened his own business. Yet for some reason unknown around town, "Jack"—as he was known—suddenly abandoned his burgeoning family and business, then disappeared. Someone later claimed he was seen in Oakland, California.

The other event that nearly crushed Dr. Miller and his wife emotionally was the double tragedy involving Dr. William Harris, the pharmacist brought from the South to manage the Miller Drug Store. A large, handsome, light-skinned man, he eventually shot to death his female clerk, then himself. The clerk, always introduced as his wife, was actually his white mistress. The legal wife of Dr. Harris, his two sons and a daughter later came to reside in Chester. A few years earlier, these largely coincidental tragedies were preceded by the unlikely suicide of William Holt, a happy-go-lucky young man. A popular basketball player, known as "Slats," and the adopted son of a professional family, he was a fixture around Miller's Drug Store, where he occasionally was employed.

These extremely unfortunate incidents happening during the war years were in reality home-front casualties, and the victims never had the opportunities to be tested for their possible positive contributions to the community in peacetime.

Role of Black Clergy Ambivalent

Whatever were the church ministers' responsibilities besides stressing the need for salvation of the souls, there were

Chapter 3

young members who viewed as equally important the material obligations owed Blacks and their community. Old-line pastors, sometimes purposely detouring slightly from their traditional sermons upon sensing youths' growing dissatisfaction with earthly, everyday problems, often would emphasize the ideals of patriotism. "Remember, the colored man never did anything to soil the American flag," the pastor would say. "Just be patient and every good will come your way. Trust in God!" At home, the young often heard, "Don't never argue about politics and religion. It causes bad friendship." From the political leaders came the admonition, "Colored folks don't pay enough taxes to make any demands."[1]

Ironically, it was in a few churches that young folks began pondering the truthfulness and practicality of such warnings. This often occurred early Sunday evenings during meetings of such groups as the Baptist Training Union, the Methodist Church Epworth League and the Allen Endeavor (AME) when some young potential leaders would substitute topics of community shortcomings in place of the standardized biblical subjects.[2] Interestingly enough, these were the periods prior to the arrival of the pastors or the conservative trustees. A partial list of the participants and their churches could indeed be recognized as future pillars of the community.

St. Daniel's Methodist: Cecil Bond, Hattie Bailey, Juanita and Maureen Murray, Rudolph Holland, Frinjella Powell, George

Four young men who came up through churches to become community leaders: Wright was a district attorney then a judge; Cameron, a minister at St. Daniel's United Methodist Church; Bond, a spark plug in the '46 school integration campaign; and Sallard, a YMCA pioneer.

From left: Robert Wright, Thomas Cameron, Cecil Bond, Joseph Sallard

Raymond, Joseph West, Nelson Bobo and Joseph Gibbs.

Asbury AME: Herman Laws, Ben Rodgers, Eugene Johnson, Clarence Maloney, Thelma Peterson and Roberta Gibbs.

Calvary Baptist: Fred Ivey, Leo Holmes, Sally Richardson, Fred Colley, Joseph Sallard, Othello Stanbeck, Isiah and Melvin Lewis.

Murphy AME: Williard Brown, Earl Carpenter, Robert Wright, Harold Smith and Thomas E. Cameron.

Bethany Baptist: Wilson Harper, Jessie Powell, Major Ellis and Jessie Edwards.

Although some went off to college and, more often than not, became schoolteachers, they undoubtedly did help inspire the coming generation. Most of the others assumed leading roles in the Black reform campaigns launched in the 1940s.

Possibly troubled lest her pastor be accused of allowing young Turks to rail against the political system that stymied community reform, a young teacher closely associated with the church hierarchy once volunteered a speech to an Epworth League session during the campaign to elect Franklin D. Roosevelt to a second term. She repeated the line proffered by the daily papers, and echoed by the local politicians: "Our children and grandchildren will have to pay for the excesses of the national Democratic administration." No doubt, the young lady ultimately saw the "light" so often referred to in the Bible. The next four decades of her illustrious career were devoted to church and school activities, plus heading up the Lucy A. Wricks Scholarship fund which aided hundreds of young folks.

Black clergymen at the time generally did not publicly involve themselves or their congregation in things political. Yet as some deacons or trustees may have secured their jobs through the influence of their GOP committeeman, a pastor's tenure might sometimes be subject to covert undercurrents.

One suspected example of that type of power could be observed in the case of the Rev. Dwight V. Kyle, a fiery young pastor assigned to Murphy AME Church in the early 1940s. His wife, Grace, was the daughter of AME Bishop R. R. Wright, and his

Chapter 3

presiding elder was the Rev. J. L. Link, a Chester resident and a force in the local NAACP prior to the young element takeover. Kyle wasted no time taking on the political figures during his appearance at community meetings. Invited once to a meeting of the Dunbar Literary Society, the jim-crow club of Chester High School, Kyle immediately began hurling a scathing denunciation at the segregated practice, and personally denounced the advisor, Leah Bloom, an English teacher who just happened to be Jewish, reminding her of her race's suffering and humiliation.

Kyle, nicknamed the "Bishop" as an undergraduate at Wilberforce College, never earned the appreciation nor confidence of his presiding elder or some of his trustees on account of similar public confrontations; and as a result his pastorate at Murphy was relatively short, despite being the son-in-law of a prominent bishop. During a tenure in Memphis, Kyle ran unsuccessfully for Congress against a candidate of the Crump machine—a clique as infamous as Chester's McClurites. His subsequent ecclesiastical charge was deep in Georgia.[3]

A directly opposite case of suspected political implications concerned the Rev. Leon S. Moore, who pastored at St. Daniel's Methodist Church for twenty-four years. Highly respected by both races, he sat on numerous interracial boards and organized a variety of community programs among his congregation, which consisted of what was believed to be a majority of the town's Black professionals. In one of these groups was the Matthew Henson Hi-Y club, which was the forerunner of the first Black YMCA. He also established a "community night" at the church, offering amateur basketball and fun games. So, when, in 1943, this prominent leader was surprisingly slated for an out-of-town assignment, speculation ran rampant as to the reason for the sudden move, just as the reform movement among Blacks was getting under way. Around town, several theories were considered:

1. Rev. Moore was beginning to lean towards either of the McClure or Pew factions girding for political control.

2. Rev. Moore and his wife, parents of two daughters and a son, were recently divorced.

3. Rev. Moore was responsible for the cadre of young reform instigators.

Yet, strangely enough, there appeared no widespread opposition expressed against the transfer. Leon Moore was succeeded by a cousin, the Rev. Noah Moore, a presiding elder from Maryland's Eastern Shore district. To the surprise of many, the new pastor opened the church doors for the first time for community mass meetings.

Two Who Survived

Positive proof, on the other hand, that forward-looking yet tactful clergymen could survive as well as thrive in a strong politically charged atmosphere may be observed in the almost simultaneous tenure of two Baptist ministers: the Reverends J. Pius Barbour of Calvary Baptist Church and D. A. Scott of Bethany Baptist Church.

Barbour, who came to the 45-year-old church in 1934, brought a demeanor and style that first caused the congregation and community to look askance, probably unaware that he was a scholar, an amateur philosopher as well as a progressive minister. Under his leadership both the church membership and the property holdings increased. However, when his pastoral duties were done for the day, one might see Rev. Barbour strolling along West Third Street, his black derby sitting at a rakish angle, sporting horn-rimmed spectacles and dangling a giant cigar between his teeth. At times he paused to chat with young folks or stood in front of the pool hall along with some of its habitues. Very often he would visit the office of Alderman Casper H. Green where local political figures frequently held court in the smoke-filled back-room. At other periods, he would be found in the library of the Crozer Theological Seminary in deep reflection on the works of Kant or Tillich.

A brother of J. Russell, editor of the *National Baptist Voice*, J. Pius never failed to pen off letters to newspapers expressing himself on various issues. Once in a local Black paper, he contributed an open letter to the young reform leaders urging them to concentrate on the school campaign only, and not scatter their shots to their other

Chapter 3

announced targets, such as transportation, theater segregation or housing.[4] In 1950, Rev. Barbour secured as his assistant pastor a young Crozer Seminary student by the name of Martin Luther King, Jr., whose dreams were possibly far too broad for the little town of Chester to encompass. Seldom getting actively involved in civic or political controversies, Barbour nevertheless maintained a friendly balance between the "Old Guard" and the "New Negro" as the leaders of the two Black factions were beginning to be characterized. So beloved was he by his parishioners that when he died in 1974 his remains were entombed in a sepulchre on his church lawn. During an anniversary memorial he was eulogized by the Rev. Marshal Shepherd, Jr., son of a long-time friend, as "one who gruffly prodded and poked the minds of other Blacks and helped them grow."[5]

Rev. Scott, who came to Bethany Baptist Church in 1940 from a Philadelphia pastorate, was more of a quiet organizer and builder than Rev. Barbour. Though his church and congregation were largely located in the "Hill" section, as the area above Ninth Street was termed, Scott soon found himself thrown pell-mell into city-wide problems and services. Unfortunately, he was obviously ill-prepared for the civic buzz-saw he encountered with his appointment to the Chester School Board. Presumably tapped for the post by John McClure or his minions as a replacement for Lewis M. Hunt in wake of the latter's domestic scandal, Scott was

Rev. Daniel Scott.

51

forced to bear a great deal of the brunt of the heated campaign for Black school reforms. Accused of not relaying their concerns to other school board members, angry parents once picketed Scott's residence as well as the targeted schools and the superintendent's office. After the court's ruling in favor of the parents, Scott eventually played a role similar to the Rev. Leon Moore's, as the Black representative on important inter-racial boards. He also served with the NAACP branch, the West End YMCA and Opportunities Industrialization Center. As president of the West End Ministerial Fellowship he was largely responsible for construction of the Martin Luther King Homes, and later a 72-unit complex dedicated as the Daniel A. Scott Commons.[6]

From a tiny congregation organized on Fulton Street in 1917, Rev. Scott guided his parishioners through several stages of buildings, culminated by a modernistic edifice at Twelfth and Tilghman Streets in 1952. One example of his diplomatic talent was illustrated by the donation of a handsome sign board in front of the new church, which was from "our mutual friend, Mr. Mack Margoline," noted Rev. Scott.[7] Margoline, ironically, was the owner of two movie houses that segregated Blacks until a few years earlier.

Like St. Daniel's Church which set an early standard in providing recreation and character-molding programs for youths, two other later churches with comparatively smaller followings initiated similar activities in the early 1930s. St. Mary's Episcopal and the Fifth Presbyterian churches evidently viewed their programs as one other means of increasing their memberships as well as their prestige in the community. Nationally, both of these denominations were predominantly white and middle-class.

Fifth Presbyterian was founded by the Rev. Thomas M. Thomas, an early graduate of Lincoln University, who later constructed a recreation center adjacent to his stone-front edifice near Third and Norris Streets. A variety of activities were carried on for neighborhood young people. After the founder-pastor retired, one of his succeeding young pastors, the Rev. H. R. Patrick, was busily involved in civic concerns during the war years, especially

Chapter 3

Rev. Thomas M. Thomas (left) and the Fifth Presbyterian Church he founded, later renamed in his honor.

the campaign for a YMCA building.

St. Mary's Episcopal Church actually began its community services centered on the youth. The Rev. A. M. Moore, the rector, organized and even participated in basketball games in the small church basement, as it provided the best space available in the community where everyone could participate without restrictions on weekday evenings. Ironically, the standard-size gym in the new Douglass School next door was not available regularly to families of tax-paying citizens.

Another congregation organized during the Depression years was the Church of God in Christ, of the Pentecostal or "holiness" denomination. Its founder was Elder Cornelius Range, a dynamic clergyman who came from Oklahoma with his wife and growing young brood. His first "church" was a fairly large circus tent on Central Avenue and Sixth Street, where services were conducted every night of the week, filling the surrounding neighborhood with joyful hymns accompanied by piano and tambourines.

Regular healing sessions were conducted by the pastor and members through the "laying on of hands" for ailing members while others spoke in "tongues" during the rituals. Range convinced congregation members to offer traditional tithes for church upkeep, and to bring canned food or groceries each Friday to help feed his family. Within a few years Range was able to purchase a Cadillac. He reportedly had previously dubbed autos

"Hell's chariots." Nonetheless, the congregation did increase and prosper to the point of building a basement-type worship quarters that eventually led to a larger edifice on the property. Eventually the congregation outgrew these quarters, almost simultaneous to the planned erection of the Lamokin Village federal housing project. The congregation's new edifice, built at Central Avenue and Second Street, would be known as "Range's Temple." The Range family, now eight strong, eventually moved to Boston where another congregation would be organized.

Church-School Youth Programs

School boys from several church-sponsored groups were also participants in another project whose aims were likewise to develop high standards of Christian character. These were the YMCA's Gra-Y clubs, two of which were carried on after regular classes, particularly at Booker T. Washington (post-1932) and Watts Elementary schools, where Henson Hi-Y members served as advisors. At every gathering prior to athletic games or serious discussions on morals and behavior, the boys recited the club motto: "Clean Speech, Clean Sports, Clean Scholarship and Clean Living." The Watts membership ranged from fourth to sixth grade; then they eventually passed on to Washington where their Gra-Y advisor was George T. Raymond, who also happened to be president of the school parent-teachers association.

In cooperation with the principal and teachers, a personal record was kept regarding the histories and attitudes of the thirty Watts club members. One positive result of this procedure was that the club placed fourth in all-round performances among the seventeen similar clubs in all Delaware County.[8] Seven years later when the survey was concluded as to the current situations of the youths, some interesting findings were discovered. Only seven of them had graduated from high school where there were 54 Blacks out of the total graduating class of 219.[9] Two of the seven gained top honors in athletics and scholastics, Lonnie McDonald and Donald Fontaine. Noah "Slick" Gethers, the first four-letter athlete in the school's history,[10] entered Morgan College on a football scholarship. Seven reached high school before dropping out, six had been transferred to classes for problem children, and the remainder quit in junior high. And not surprisingly, 80 percent of the youths had been raised in "broken" homes where there was either only one parent or a common-law arrangement. Among other student participants in the 1938 Gra-Y program were Commodore Harris, Wilmer Woodland, Charles Terry, Melvin Kennedy, Albert McDuffy, Charles Goldsby, Thomas Pitts, Benny Wright, Pierce Stansbury, Arthur Bean, James Spence, George Elzy, Solomon Johnson and George Miller.

One particular case stood out glaringly. It seemed an example of poor judgment on the part of school personnel in dealing with Roscoe Harris, one of the former Gra-Y boys from Watts School. He was an excellent athlete and showed some natural musical talent. He resided with his sister and mother, a domestic worker. Though far from being a brilliant student he managed to pass on to junior high school, yet was later transferred to a school for "slow learners." He was eventually expelled from that school for attempting to protect a younger pupil being pummeled by the instructor. Shortly afterwards, expressing interest in earning enough money to enter a music school, Roscoe joined the Navy.

Unfortunately, he was one of the many sailors that died in the Fort Chicago tragedy during the war. True, this was an isolated incident in which death was the end result of one's attempt to rise above his environment, but Roscoe's mother later said, "I am more satisfied that he died in honor of his country, and did not bring disgrace on his family, as I have seen some of his former playmates do."

SOUTH CHESTER, A THRIVING COMMUNITY
Bibliography

1. R. E. Harris, *Delinquency In Our Democracy* (Philadelphia: Wetzel Publishing, 1954), p. 21.

2. Ibid, p. 22.

3. Ibid, p. 86.

4. Delaware County *Crusader* newspaper, June 15, 1946.

5. *Philadelphia Inquirer*, February 17, 1984, p. 4-B.

6. *Delaware County Daily Times*, December 16, 1973.

7. 70th Anniversary booklet of Bethany Baptist Church, 1947.

8. Harris, *Delinquency*, p. 26.

9. *Crusader*, June 8, 1946.

10. Harris, *Delinquency*, p. 25.

Chapter 4

Segregated Schools Finally Targeted (1936-40)

INADEQUATE CURRICULA PROTESTED; JIM-CROW HIGH SCHOOL BLOCKED

With the exception of the Booker T. Washington building constructed in 1923, and the Frederick Douglass in 1932, all Black schools were more than a half century old, and at various times condemned as unsanitary and/or fire hazards. In all cases, over-crowdedness was generally applicable to those ancient buildings.

As Black students increased in both the Seventeenth Street and lower Market Street areas, a few of the old down-own buildings were reopened as segregated schools. Among those were Harvey, built in 1867 as the city's first high school; Hoskins (1882), formerly the city tax collector's office; and Gartside (1870), reopened to accommodate "backward" Black students. Only two schools were previously designated exclusively for all Blacks—George Jones at Seventeenth and Walnut Streets, and John A. Watts at Fourth and Edwards in south Chester. Third grade pupils from Jones went

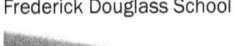

Frederick Douglass School

to Harvey, Fifth and Welsh Streets, for fourth through the sixth grades. From Harvey, all pupils, including those residing in the Seventeenth Street section, had to trudge approximately seven miles to matriculate in the Black junior high school at Seventh Street and Central, passing the "white" Smedley Junior High. Even worse, those north Chester students reaching the ninth grade had to pass Chester High School which ordinarily housed that grade through the twelfth.[1]

Thanks to a few determined parents, this was the situation causing the first serious challenge to school authorities. When the new Frederick Douglass School opened, the school board purposely omitted giving it any specific designation, obviously to conceal its covert attempt to establish a completely Black high school. The June 1932 class graduating from Booker T. Washington Junior High was instructed by authorities to report to Douglass for tenth grade classes rather than to Chester High. The resultant objections from numerous Black parents were loud and clear with charges of discrimination and segregation. The local NAACP branch, then under control of teachers and other professionals, did routinely protest the action. Yet it was a handful of parents led by Mrs. Mary Murray that boldly escorted their new tenth grade children to Chester High School daily, only to see them refused registration and admittance.

A few civic leaders later sought to use moral suasion on school authorities to no avail; and since the NAACP took no legal action against the board, parents—realizing their children were losing so much time without getting an education—called off their campaign. A few sent their children to out-of-town schools while the rest returned to Douglass.

Maureen Murray Roberts, now a retired teacher, recalled the trying ordeal. "Finally, mother arranged for me to live with friends in Philadelphia and attend William Penn High School, from which I graduated. Several others, including Rosa Hunt and Janester Nicholas also attended high schools out of town." However, authorities ultimately relented, giving the junior high school designation to Douglass, but ruled that Black students would enter Chester High at the tenth grade level, rather than the

Chapter 4

ninth.

Black students in those times lacked adequate career counseling in any of the secondary classes, and thus were generally unable to decide upon reaching Chester High as to which of the four curricula to pursue—college preparatory, general, commercial or industrial. For instance, of the 24 Blacks graduating in the 1938 class of 219, the majority took the general course, and only three finished the college preparatory. For quite obvious reasons, none took the industrial or commercial courses! First of all, neither of those two courses were offered at Douglass; and to pursue one or the other, a student would be forced to sacrifice an entire school year to be able to catch up. Another sensible rationale for foregoing either course—industrial or commercial—was the low possibility of a Black gaining local employment commensurate with such training, simply due to the widespread discrimination in the work force in the area.

In 1943, Douglass School again became the center of another controversy involving the community and the school board—this time for the latter's failure to consider two local teachers for a "newly created post" at the school. A Washington, D.C. professional was recommended by board member Lewis M. Hunt for the position that was classified as a counselor, but it was learned the successful applicant would actually be successor to William K. Valentine, soon to retire as Douglass principal. Because this was not necessarily a matter of racial discrimination, what with several political leaders supporting Hunt's candidate, members of the Independent Civic League, some also holding key offices in the local NAACP, launched a campaign to have either James H. Grasty or Leon J. Hill, both teachers with masters' degrees, considered for the position. The usual political persuasion ultimately won over, for neither of the presumably qualified Douglass instructors were selected. The new principal of Douglass would be Beverly Y. Blow, who had often served as Mr. Valentine's unofficial assistant. Blow, like Grasty and Hill, was also a Lincoln graduate, whose mother had been a local teacher.

In times past, small town school principals ordinarily were expected to set examples to inspire incentive and discipline and

Politics and Prejudice

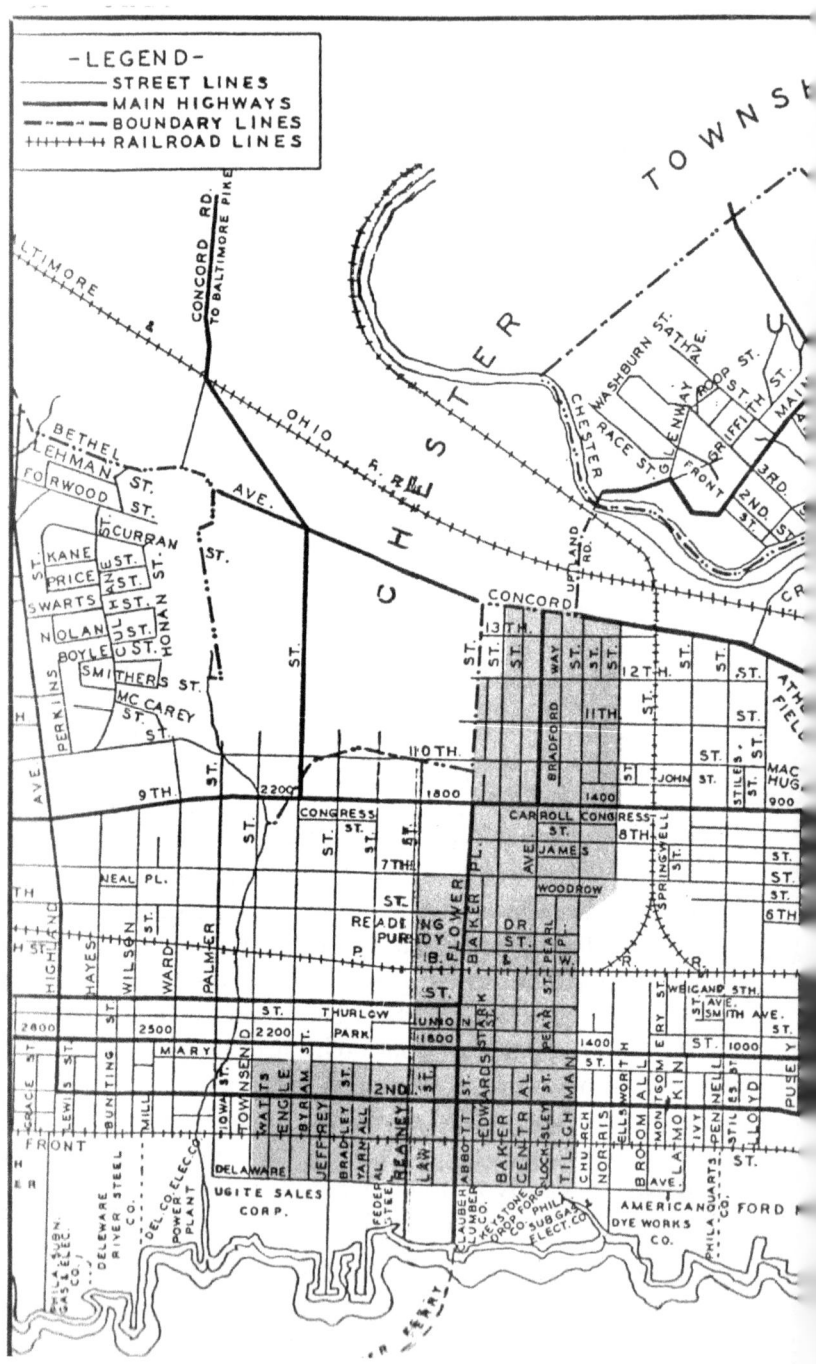

Shaded areas indicate Black neighborhoods, 1930-1950.

Chapter 4

Politics and Prejudice

Left: James Grasty. Right: Catherine Brown Laws.

to see that their staff helped motivate pupils in the hope they would grow to become productive citizens. One of the earliest professionals of this calibre was none other than Mrs. Carrie M. Pipes, the long-time principal at Watts School.

Later, it was William K. Valentine at both Booker T. Washington and Douglass, and his eventual successor at BTWS, Miss Catherine Brown. Then what seemed a game of musical chairs, Grasty, who resigned after his rejection for the top post at Douglass, eventually returned to Chester as principal at Watts. Moreover, it seemed a curious case of extreme irony that Grasty's Watts School would become the launching pad for a grass-roots explosion that eventually spread city-wide for the first time in its history.

It could be said in retrospect that these four pedagogues and their immediate charges were responsible for exerting varying amounts of influence on the lives of several generations of Black citizens for a half century.

Mr. Valentine, whose teaching career began sometime prior to 1916, carried on his duties until his retirement in 1944. Professor or "Fess" (as he was nicknamed out of his earshot by students)

Chapter 4

was a light-complexioned man slightly resembling Theodore Roosevelt sans a mustache. The affable schoolman, on the other hand, who always referred to students as "my children," was a bachelor whose elderly mother resided with him in their Flower Street residence. Ever bubbling with enthusiasm, he always attended the school's athletic contests. Each morning at opening assemblies he read from the Bible, his favorite being the thirteenth chapter of Corinthians: "Though I speak with the tongues of men and of angels and have not love I am become as sounding brass, or a tinkling cymbal.... And now abideth Faith, Hope and Love, these three; but the greatest of these is Love." On each Wednesday assembly, he encouraged a music appreciation hour, during which primarily classical records were played by James Grasty who offered personal comment on each number.

Succeeding Mr. Valentine as principal at Booker T. was Catherine Brown. Born in Tuckahoe, Maryland, she became a teacher at Watts after graduating from West Chester Teachers College. In a union that shortly afterwards brought together two of the highly respected role models for Black youth, she and Herman Laws were married. He had completed his Army stint and now served as counselor at both Washington and Douglass schools. Mrs. Laws, after serving twenty-four years in the school system, decided to retire and pursue another career.

Why would a woman so well-respected and admired want to forsake her original calling, was the question posed by many who thought they knew her very well.

"We were disgusted with the school system," she was later quoted. "Teaching is hard, hard work, if you are interested in the welfare of the children. I was a teaching principal, and trying to do that job alone was horrendous. Frankly, I left education for two reasons—there wasn't enough money in it and there weren't enough teachers to do the right job."[2] At that time, local teachers' wages ranged from $1,000 to $1,800, it was learned.

Unfortunately, the school system and the Black community both lost two important leaders in a short span of time. Herman Laws, not in the best of health since doing his military service, died in 1953, a year or so after both he and his wife had embarked on new fields of endeavor.

Blacks' Experiences at CHS

What was it like for Blacks attending a completely white-dominated Chester High where there wasn't even a Black custodian to discuss problems with? One youth, who became disillusioned and dropped out, expressed his feelings this way: "In elementary and junior high schools our teachers seldom expressed anything about Black pride and accomplishments. Race-wise, we were living in a vacuum, no record of the past, and no barometer for the future. So, once in high school, we had little chance to compete with white students. Yet, deep down, we knew that all whites were neither smarter or faster than all colored kids, but we never got much chance to prove it."

No Blacks indeed were accepted in extra-curricular groups, so doubtlessly as a paternalistic gesture, the Chester High faculty organized the "Dunbar Literary Society" expressly for the Blacks. The "society," which had a white advisor, actually never dealt with anything "literary." The main event of the group was an annual dance which the administration financed.

The male students formed their own football aggregation, choosing the name "Dunbar A. C.," not particularly to claim association with the "literary society," but because the Douglass and Booker T. Washington schools had already laid claims to the names of their other best-known heroes. The squad selected their own coach from among their best players, bought their own equipment and furnished their own transportation to compete with Black teams in Wilmington, Coatesville, Downingtown, Philadelphia and other nearby towns.

Most of the Dunbar squad seemed to look forward with equal anticipation to the frequent practice scrimmages with the Chester High varsity team. The meetings were anything but friendly get-togethers between white and Black classmates. The Dunbar boys boasted of playing much harder against the Orange and Black team whose coach was Babe Buono, a product of the exclusive Pennsylvania Military College.

Prior to Buono's tenure, the athletic coach Charles "Pard" Larkin

Chapter 4

had encouraged such natural performers as Ted Graham in track and Henry "Alex" Hunt in football to help boost CHS teams to victories. Also during that period of time the girls' varsity team included a few Blacks, including Margaret Loper, Dorothy Moore and Helen Money.

For the increased number of boys who later made the high school varsity teams, much credit could be due to the encouragement and preparation gotten from their junior high coaches. One of "Jim" Grasty's proteges at Booker T., Herbert "Stardust" Norris, was the only Black selected for the all-suburban football team in 1933 as a guard on the high school squad. Norris later starred on Lincoln University's grid aggregation. London B. Jones, the new Douglass first coach tutored several youths later starring at Chester High, including Talbot Green, Leamon Bowen and Noah Gethers.

In basketball at Chester High, Cecil Bond was the first of several Blacks to make it, followed by three Floyd brothers at different school years—James, Edward and John. Incidentally, if an independent club in the community ever wanted to field a mixed team, it could have been the "Floyd Five," as two sisters, Veora and Pecolia, also won their letters in high school.

Possibly for the lack of role models in other realms, numerous athletes and sports figures tended to be held in rather high esteem, especially in Chester's Black community. Regarding this assumption, one could mention Henry "Alex" Hunt and his wife, Helen Money Hunt, James H. Grasty, Richard N. Thomas and Gethers, who was elected Ninth Ward constable upon returning to Chester following a brief career as a Morgan State College grid standout.

Judging from the stellar performances demonstrated over the years by players with such local grid aggregations as the Comet A. C., Dunbar A. C. or Central Boys Club, a current belief existed among some sports enthusiasts why so few Black youths were unwilling to demonstrate their talents at Chester High. The conclusions: not enough confidence in themselves; unwillingness to go through the strict, rigorous training schedule; and inability to maintain their academic eligibility. Even candidates failing to pass scholastically were willing to vouch for the fairness among

Politics and Prejudice

the new order of coaches, particularly Ollie Robinson (football) and George Lang (track) who arrived in the mid-1930s.

SEGREGATED SCHOOLS FINALLY TARGETED
Bibliography

1. 64th Annual Commencement Program of Chester High School, 1938.

2. *Delaware County Daily Times,* July 22, 1987.

Chapter 5

War Years Create A Boom-Town (1941-45)

INDUSTRY BRINGS BENEFITS TO NEGROES; POLITICAL FACTIONS BATTLE

As a middle-sized industrialized town low on cultural and educational offerings, especially for its Black population, Chester suddenly experienced some wrenching episodes during the Second World War and its immediate aftermath. It was, moreover, a period in which Blacks saw an opportunity to challenge the political system through events that eventually would reap some hard-earned benefits.

Sun Shipbuilding and Dry Dock, one of the area's largest employers, which previously hired Blacks only as common laborers, announced early in 1942 the establishment of a separate unit to build tankers under a government contract as part of the war effort.[1] Most surprising, however, was that the new "Number 4 Yard" would be operated exclusively by Blacks. Unfortunately for local Blacks, virtually none ever had opportunities for any skilled, semi-skilled or technical training, so hundreds had to be recruited and transported in. A great majority of these new workers consequently were prepared under a federal defense program, the Engineering, Science and Management War Training Program, operated by the WPA and NYA in scores of Black colleges in the South. These young adults, male and female, were trained in ship-building and allied trades, including electrical, radio, welding and similar skills.[2]

Even though this "revolutionary" policy of the shipyard owner, John G. Pew, Sr., a prominent national GOP financier, may have appeared to be a godsend to thousands of jobless or underemployed, it was nevertheless quickly condemned by the national office of the NAACP as discriminatory. Thus, the president of the local branch, Herman Laws, who originally heralded the Pew move, was forced by the national body to retract his laudatory statements concerning the jim-crow industrial unit.

As top administrator of the No. 4 Yard, the owners announced

Dr. Emmett J. Scott
Courtesy Library of Congress, Prints & Photographs Division, George Grantham Bain Collection, Reproduction number LC-DIG-ggbain-03299.

the incongruous appointment of Dr. Emmett J. Scott, holder of an illustrious record as a statesman since his early days as a close confidant of Booker T. Washington, founder of Tuskegee Institute.[3] During his times with the great educator, Scott, a one-time newspaperman, helped Washington to exert varying influence over Black organizations, newspapers and Republican patronage appointments. He later served as a special assistant to the secretary of war during the First World War, monitoring the treatment of Black soldiers. He also authored a book, *Negro Migrations During World War I*. Just prior to being tapped for the Sun Ship post, Scott was assistant public relations director for the national Republican party, writing a free weekly column for interested Black papers.

The hidden agenda for Scott's unlikely selection was revealed to a reporter of the weekly *Philadelphia Independent* by two staffers of the War Production Board, Reginald Johnson and Clarence H. Mitchell, the future NAACP bigwig. They alleged that the Pews, powerful king-makers and owners of both the Sun Shipyard and Sun Oil companies, planned to capitalize on the shipyard venture

Chapter 5

by ultimately organizing thousands of new workers and their families—with the invaluable expertise of Dr. Scott—to wrestle control from the McClure city-county political machine.[4] The actual reason for the Pews' intended disassociation from the McClure faction was not explained publicly, yet for years McClure was believed to have enjoyed a working relationship with Pew, even to the point of sending applicants to other Pew-controlled firms in the area. The squeaky-clean Pews were certainly aware of McClure's bootlegging conviction.

"What Chester Makes, McClure Takes" became a longtime joke around town, doubtlessly referring to the more recent episode of McClure's selling the Chester Water Company to a private concern. The parody was a play on the giant lighted sign standing along the Delaware River proclaiming "WHAT CHESTER MAKES, MAKES CHESTER."

Scott's primary value to Pew's political plans were obviously in the field of public relations. Over the years he had personally known and campaigned for Republican presidents from Taft to Hoover. Quite paradoxically, he seldom, if ever, carried the political campaign or his own personal prestige to Blacks in south Chester. On the other hand, his assistant, Jerome "Brud" Holland, the personable ex-Cornell grid star, often spent time involving himself with Hi-Y and Gray-Y activities in the area.

A Scott public relations coup was fairly evident in 1943 when a little-known group, the Association of Negroes in American Industry, cited John G. Pew, Sr. with the Booker T. Washington Award "for outstanding achievement in industrial employment of Negroes."[5] Scott's friend, Bishop David H. Sims of the Eastern District of the AME Church, made the presentation to Pew, who replied, "All our workers are getting equal pay for equal work and we are greatly pleased with the work being rendered."[6] Thanks to the Shipbuilders Union's activities in the yard, no other wage scale would be tolerated.

Anyhow, as the war efforts lifted the local economy from the lean days of the dying Depression, industrial employment quickly tripled overall from approximately 14,000 to 43,000, and jobs among Blacks naturally rose, including 14,000 at Sun Ship. Other companies also engaged in defense contracts, including Sun Oil, Baldwin Locomotive, Ford Motor and several steel manufacturers that added Blacks to their payrolls, though few possessed the new skills of Black shipyard workers. Ford, which moved one of its plants to Chester in 1929 and hired only a few Black janitors, now had an interracial work force that turned out 150 army tanks and other vehicles in the 1942-45 period. Contrasting its national policy, Ford had obviously followed "local policy" until wartime.

Pews Plan Black YMCA

Whatever their true beliefs in the human dignity of man, the Pews no doubt had been long consistent, particularly in Chester, in their desires to maintain the separation of races, particularly concerning any undertaking where they planned to pour their finances. They could, of course, always sugarcoat their motives. Divided work forces in industry were duplicated in plans to separate Black and white members in the Young Men's Christian Association. The 1946 election year was nearly three years hence, yet Sun Ship owners unveiled a project carrying the dubious elements of politics and race relations. Through their associates, the Pews announced plans to partially underwrite two new YMCA buildings; one for Blacks in south Chester, the second to replace the main Y headquarters in the city business district. Both buildings would be completed simultaneously, it was promised.[7] In the meantime, Black members of Y groups could continue their monthly visits on their "guest night" recreation at the main YMCA. On one occasion, the YMCA Director Emory O. Nelson, while lecturing to young Black guests, began telling a joke about an "old nigger—I mean colored man..." he quickly corrected. When Nelson learned later that a Gra-Y advisor accompanying the group reported the incident to the *Pittsburgh Courier*'s Philadelphia edition, he vigorously denied the remark.[8]

The Y campaign planners did not contact or consult with any of the young men who for years had carried the torch for the movement. Instead, they chose an "executive committee" from among a few Black professionals and political figures not usually associated with character-building for the youth. Reluctant at first to accept what they considered subordinate roles in the fund-raising

Chapter 5

drive, the Gra-Y advisors and Hi-Y members eventually relented and participated wholeheartedly. After a whirlwind, ten-day campaign in the summer of 1943, $23,000 was raised, topping the set goal of $15,000 as the half-share of the Black YMCA building. The entire operation, presided over by a representative of the Y national headquarters, was composed of ten 5-member teams and a "big gift" committee, consisting of the Reverends J. P. Barbour, L. J. Link, L. R. Patrick and D. A. Scott; Doctors L. H. Hardy, W. H. Henderson, L. McNight and W. E. Smith; businessmen L. M. Hunt, R. Prince, George Nugent and J. S. Hunt; political figures Richard Thomas and Casper H. Green; educators W. K. Valentine and J. H. Grasty; and Y advisors Joseph S. West and Joseph Sallard.[9]

During the wrap-up session at the Harlem Hotel, a former lodge hall for whites, Richard Thomas keynoted an appeal "for the oneness of purpose" between two hitherto generally recognized factions of community leadership as typified by most members of the executive committee and team members. He concluded, "Together we can be the controlling power in the city, socially, politically or by any other means. We must stick together and make Chester what it should be." David Nelson Bobo, Jr., the youngest team captain whose team raised the highest amount of pledges, responded, declaring, "We want to be included in everything with you elders. We do not necessarily want to be included in your social activities, but in all political affairs. Just give us a chance!"[10]

A recruited skilled ship-yard employee.

71

Politics and Prejudice

WEST END YMCA BOARD OF DIRECTORS. (Front row, from left) Lorenzo Thompson; Henry (Alex) Hunt; unidentified Central YMCA staff member; Emory Nelson, Central YMCA Executive Director; Dr. Larney Hardy; Rev. J. L. Link. (Back row, from left) Harry Swiggett; Hartford Showell; John F. L. Reason, West End YMCA Director; Joseph S. Hunt; Joseph Sallard; Joseph S. West; and Joseph Kane.

However, this pledge of cooperation was, in a sense, short-lived. When time came to select a permanent board of managers for the contemplated project, the majority of team members voted out several known politicians and others with no prior relations with youth programs. This maneuver indeed represented the first open contention between the two Black factions, guaranteed to continue for at least a decade or so. The new West End YMCA (the official name) board finally consisted of a workable merger of the "New Negro," the "Old Guard" and a few middle-of-the-road professionals.

John F. L. Reason, a veteran youth worker from West Chester, was hired as executive director of the building-less West End Y, conducting his business mainly from an office in the main YMCA building. Local churches and schools provided space needed for some programs, and a rubble-strewn lot near the Pennsylvania Railroad tracks was cleared to provide a temporary athletic field.

The reason given for the holdup of Y construction plans was that wartime requirements for various building materials constituted

Chapter 5

CENTRAL BOYS CLUB FOOTBALL TEAM. The squad coached by Henry (Alex) Hunt, far right. The organization tried in vain to secure the USO building as its headquarters. (Photo by Frederick "Jim" Douglass)

a national priority. Yet a $250,000 all-purpose USO building was begun at Eighth Street and Central during the war and completed after V.J. Day, 1945.[11] In the absence of the promised West End YMCA, some community factions began an informal campaign to secure the USO complex as a recreation center. Besides its gym, the building was supplied with modern furniture, meeting rooms, kitchen equipment, refrigeration and stoves, among other conveniences. However, all efforts to purchase or lease the facilities failed. [12]

A few years later, white businesses were in competition to get the building, each for a different purpose. One firm offered the Federal Works Administration as much as $50,000 for the structure, which would then be either demolished and sold as surplus or used as a warehouse. The FWA agent, joking at what he considered a too-low offer, said, "I am thinking about running over to Philly to find out if Father Divine would like to buy a building." Seriously, he added that a nonprofit, public organization might be able to get the property for much less than a private purchaser, or could secure it through a lease. Suddenly, to the surprise of many, city building inspector James Devlin declared the USO complex an unsafe fire hazard when filled with people.[13] He furthermore added that under the Landham Act, such temporary constructions were supposed to be removed at the war's end. In the period between the completion and the eventual razing, a "Farmers' Market" was

Politics and Prejudice

Two examples of deteriorated housing.

permitted to occupy and conduct business in the building.

Housing Shortage Critical

Even when Housing Authority Director George Mitchell estimated in 1943 that Blacks accounted for one-third of the city population, they had no chance of occupying that percentage of the housing. Consequently, with war-workers and their families still streaming in, housing shortages shoved Blacks into desperate straits. Housing codes among realtors, written or not, prevented them from renting, leasing or purchasing abodes in white neighborhoods, regardless of their economic positions. Making matters worse, the establishment powers seldom failed in their attempts to discourage any more home construction for low-income families.

A review of the 1940 U.S. Census on housing did offer concrete evidence of local Blacks' inability to obtain more decent family accommodations. Of the 14,834 housing units in Chester, Blacks occupied only 2,437. In the Ninth Ward, center of their residencies where 4,650 lived, they occupied 980 units, of which 488 had no private baths or were in need of major repairs. Of these homes, 136 were built in 1899 or earlier, 227 in the 1900-19 period, and 213 in the 1920-30 decade. Overall, 35% of the city's housing units were constructed in 1899 or earlier and 49% in the 1900-19 period.[14]

Similar conditions existed in 1937-38 at the time the McClure faction launched a secret all-out offensive against the national administration's slum-clearance housing plans scheduled for Chester. One incredible ploy had one of the local henchmen

Chapter 5

spreading reports that residents of the contemplated federal housing would be forced to turn off electricity and radios at nine o'clock every evening.

When the political bosses manipulated to have control of all the jobs involved, 1,050 units of slum-clearance housing were allowed the green-light. The units were divided into three projects of nearly equal living quarters. Lamokin Village, split by Central Avenue where a number of businesses had thrived for years, was exclusively for Blacks. The other two projects, McCaffrey Village, in the Highland Avenue area and the William Penn were for whites, although 400 Blacks had been displaced to make way for the latter project.[15]

The eventual selection of Joseph S. Hunt, a local contractor, as Lamokin Project director, came as a surprise to many. Not previously associated with any particular political group, he was generally believed to have been a compromise among the McClures, Democrats, and the Pews. Relatively progressive in his outlook, Hunt (no relation to Lewis M. Hunt) inaugurated constructive programs in the Village, including organizing a community day-care center for working mothers.

Not surprisingly, opposition flared again when it was learned that under the war emergency Landham Act, 150 temporary homes would be constructed a few blocks south of Lamokin Village. Even though it was known publicly the units would be demolished at war's end, a white citizens committee went to court in a move to kill the plan, but their request was rejected. After these emergency quarters were in place, more homes for Black war-workers were so badly needed that many were renting garages and basements for sleeping quarters.

One more effort to create critically needed housing came from the Joseph Day Company of New York, sponsor of similar housing across the nation.[16] The general prospectus of the plan gained editorial support of the daily *Chester Times* which had recently come under more liberal ownership. The Day representative, Beulah Fritz, following extensive surveys and planning, developed four tentative blueprints and applied to the Federal Housing Authority for approval of a single one. The first three were rejected, reported as being too close to slum areas already inhabited by Blacks. The local FHA agent contended the fourth proposed site would be too remote from school and transportation facilities.[17] Thus no more housing would be available for Black defense employees.

Robert C. Weaver, one of the nation's leading authorities on housing, later wrote about the Chester matter: "The more the proposed site was compared with other acceptable sites," he stated, "the more one was forced to conclude that it was far superior in location, topography and access to existing facilities than most of those in which FHA had insured mortgages."

"There were inevitable deficiencies on most sites under wartime conditions of shortages, and general inadequacies in schools and transportation," he continued.[18]

Mrs. Fritz, who had kept Black leaders apprised of her progress, later said "a large, influential financial institution had invested heavily in housing for whites near the favored site, and had pressured the local FHA office not to approve" the Day project.[19]

Boom-Town Ills Felt Deeply

By now, the town was rapidly becoming something of a boom-town, though not quite as undisciplined as those in the old West, yet law enforcement was wholly inadequate and often inefficient. Just as in most areas of rapidly increasing demands of labor, there were those who would grab more than their share of good times, spending their idle hours boozing, fighting and, in general, hell-raising. Moreover, the absence of any wholesome, organized recreation invariably contributed to the rampant disorderliness. Of the approximately one hundred city policemen, only seven or eight were Blacks whose beats were generally confined to south Chester where a great deal of the defense workers converged during their off-hours.

The Black policemen, Edward Handy, Ellery Purnsley, Dewey Kieffer, Levi Griffin, Leroy Richardson, John Reed and Oakley Berry, patrolled in two-man teams, sometimes in squad cars. Handy and Purnsley appeared more easygoing and friendly as a twosome. Handy, in fact, was often greeted as "Sarge" in the community, reflecting the fact that many felt he was deserving of

Chapter 5

a sergeant's position because of his seniority and the respect he held in the Black community. On reflection, there were those who felt they owed him a debt of gratitude because he never failed to chase away youthful gangs who gathered on street corners in the evening, though he knew his aging legs had their limitations. "If you hadn't been chasing us," one of the gang members, now an adult, told him once, "Sarge, no telling where we would be today—in prison or dead."

With the wartime industries going at full blast (most at three daily shifts), scores of south Chester residents found themselves sorely in need of adequate transportation, especially as many of the plants were located outside city limits. Baldwin Locomotive, for example, was located in Eddystone, as was a portion of Sun Shipyard. Sun Oil and Atlantic Refining were in Marcus Hook. City buses, operated exclusively by white drivers, traveled through the full lengths of Second, Third and part of Seventh Streets, yet there were no public bus lines to the "Hill" area at the ends of the main thoroughfares that consisted mainly of Tilghman, Flower and Central. Adjacent to the city's western boundaries was Chester Township and its Fairgrounds Housing Project from which elderly residents as well as defense workers had to trek to main city bus routes.

Theodore Roberts, a civic leader, accompanied by representatives of the NAACP, the Fairgrounds Housing Project Residents Association and the Progressive Men's Association conferred several times with officials of the Southeastern Pennsylvania Transportation Authority about providing bus service to the "Hill." They were finally told that such additional services "would not be a paying proposition."[20] At least two other attempts to secure adequate transportation for South Chester residents went down in failure. A group of Black veterans seeking to organize a taxicab franchise was rejected by the Pennsylvania Utilities Commission, as was a request to the local Yellow Cab concession to employ Black drivers.

In a way, all these rejections were good news for the jitney services being provided by scores of Black car owners who reaped a fairly good living from their efforts. As a consequence, news of the rebuffs only encouraged more car owners to begin offering the illicit jitney services; and when authorities threatened crackdowns, the operators allowed passengers to volunteer a "donation" for their rides. It would thus be virtually impossible for authorities to make a case against the drivers who ordinarily carried only passengers with whom they were acquainted.

Yellow Cab owners who, in view of this situation, must have suddenly gotten second thoughts regarding their obvious loss of business, eventually announced the hiring of their first Black driver, Russell Reading, son of politico Albert A. Reading. Later, the Chester franchise hired three more Black drivers, Ollie Crews, Edward Burd and Howard Collier, plus five mechanics.[21] Three permanent cab stands were established for the first time at Third and Flower, Ninth and Central Avenue, and Third and Market Streets, near the main shopping center.

Young community activists were reluctantly experiencing the dog days of the 1944 winter season. Finished was the excitement of the YMCA campaign, though no one knew if the blueprints were yet drawn. Practically everyone who wanted one, had a job in these

Benn/Roxie Theater, which became St. Luke's Christian Church; it is now Centro Cristiano Monte Sinai.

Chapter 5

bustling wartime days. Breadwinners with family responsibilities found little or no time to unwind. There was a dearth of wholesome entertainment to look forward to, as no worthwhile facilities were available to accommodate spectators or audiences. The Benn Theater, later the Roxie movie house, was converted to a church and the old fairgrounds athletic field was being covered by project homes. For a taste of night life, only Jack Farrell's Moonglow Cafe and its floor show were inviting to Blacks. Or if anyone felt adventurous enough, there was the ancient "No. 37" Toonerville-like trolley which could rock and roll all the way to Philadelphia for a variety of leisure-time pursuits.

In their spare time, a group of young men sat around in one of their Third Street hangouts reminiscing about their boyhood pals serving in, or who had died in, military service. One of the most colorful casualties in their viewpoint was Jim Nichols. "What a character!" they all agreed. Jim lived in Upland, about 10 miles from West Third Street, yet every night after hanging out with his friends, he would jog all the way home, regardless of the hour or whether dressed in his "Sunday-go-to-meeting" attire. Once when four former high school track team members were bragging about their abilities, Jim challenged them with a team he promised to produce for a contest at the Fairground, a halfway point for both groups to meet. At the appointed hour, Jim showed up, alone. "Where's your team, Jimbo?" he was asked. "Well, I couldn't get them together," he explained, then pausing, he added, "I'm here and I'm gonna take on all of you."

He meant the 100-yard dash, the broad jump, the high jump and the two-mile run. Fortunately for his competition, Jim soon got the chance to show his talent for the latter event. He spotted a runaway horse being chased by his owner who seemed pooped. Really an all-around athlete, Jim immediately took off after the animal. Nearly a half hour later Jim was seen trotting back from the chase with the exhausted nag in tow. "If the old Devil tried to catch Jimbo, he'd be lost," someone cracked during the belated wake for the spirit of a lovable young man.

Shortly afterwards someone began telling of an incident at the draft induction center: A local lad actually named General Jacobs was waiting to be called for his examination when a voice suddenly boomed out, "General Jacobs!" Every uniformed person in the place snapped to attention, ready to salute the "general." Responding to the call, however, was the real General, hardly five feet tall, zoot-suit, elevator heels and all. For a while he was completely flabbergasted at the snickering among sideline civilians, aware of the faux pas. Another youngster chimed in, "Say, we colored people got first names like General, Major, Colonel and Corporal, but we ain't got no privates." A second one in the booth nearby turned and mischievously asked, "Who ain't?"

WAR YEARS CREATE A BOOM-TOWN
Bibliography

1. *New York Times*, May 27, 1942.

2. J. H. Franklin, *From Slavery To Freedom* (New York: Alfred Knopf, 1947), p. 592.

3. *New York Times*, June 7, 1942.

4. Philadelphia Independent newspaper, June 17, 1942.

5. *New York Times*, April 29, 1943.

6. Ibid.

7. R. E. Harris, *Delinquency In Our Democracy* (Philadelphia: Wetzel Publishing, 1954), p. 23.

8. *Pittsburgh Courier* newspaper, September 12, 1937.

9. *Chester Times*, August 16, 1943.

10. Ibid.

11. Harris, *Delinquency*, p. 24.

12. Ibid.

13. *Chester Times*, September 21, 1947.

14. 1940 U.S. Census on Housing.

15. Harris, *Delinquency*, pp. 30-31.

16. Robert C. Weaver, *The Negro Ghetto* (New York: Harcourt, Brace, 1947), P. 119.

17. Harris, *Delinquency*, p. 31.

18. Weaver, *Negro Ghetto*, p. 120.

19. As related to the author.

20. *Crusader*, June 14, 1946.

21. Ibid, May 14, 1946.

Chapter 6

Postwar Era Sparks Civic Awakening (1946-50)

FIRST BLACK NEWSPAPER LEADS GRASS-ROOTS CRUSADE FOR REFORMS

The burgeoning Black population was long in need of some reliable medium for bettering communications among themselves. They certainly were well aware of the shabby treatment traditionally foisted upon them. However, the average resident was uncertain of any lawful alternatives that might be available to them, without the risk of some sort of retaliation from the domineering system.

Among those residing in other Delaware County communities isolated miles from south Chester there also existed a desire for an instrument aimed at bringing together all the groups in a common bond. Few, if any, could be expected to put much stock in reports spread by self-serving political leaders, nor the frequent newspaper stories concerning specific welfare of the race.

As the war began winding down, plans were being drawn up to publish the town's first Black newspaper. The chief organizer had earlier served two separate stints as a correspondent for the local daily *Chester Times*, and had recently resigned as city editor of the *Philadelphia Afro-American* newspaper.

Of the several public persons that were under consideration as probable partners in the journalist's venture, five were finally agreed on as admittedly being in concert with the paper's stated editorial policy and its business prospectus.

These would comprise the Board of Directors who provided the initial financing: L. M. Hardy, a dentist, and J. H. Henderson, a physician, both late-comers to town who had apparently demonstrated their civic interest and leadership potential in the Black YMCA campaign. The others were Joseph S. Hunt, a general contractor; Isiah Lewis, a young man who came up through church groups and later was president of the Douglass School PTA; and Lester Reading, a print shop owner. and estranged brother of the McClure satrap, Albert A.

Chapter 6

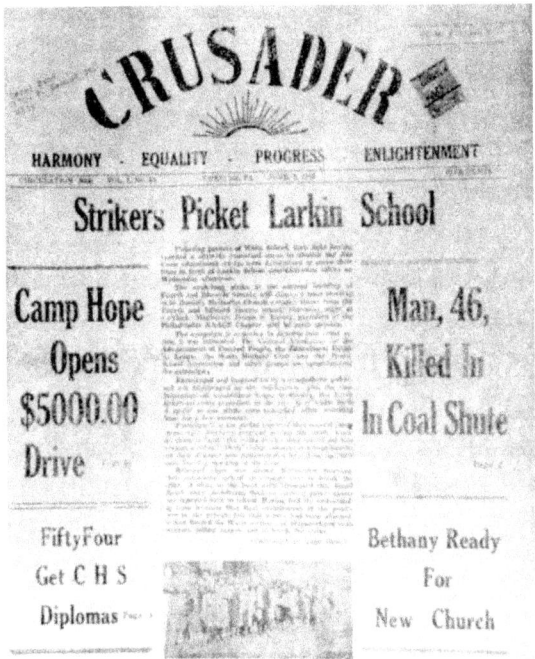

Copy of *Crusader*.

On October 6, 1945, the first edition of the weekly *Crusader* newspaper rolled off Reading's ancient flat-bed press. Its front-page editorial, printed in large type, announced a solemn pledge to "help make the home-front more pleasant and receptive for our returning GI's who went off to fight against bigotry and oppression." The 12-page tabloid was quite appropriately named the *Crusader*, simply because that was precisely what it intended to be. The masthead listed as its objectives Harmony, Equality, Progress and Enlightenment. Its immediate goals were More Adequate Housing, Improved School Facilities, Health and Sanitation Reforms, Increased Police Services, Broader Recreation Programs, Encouragement of Black Businesses, Upholding the U.S. Constitution and the State Equal Rights Bill.[1]

Aside from the core of paper boys to peddle it in the streets and deliver it to homes, the paper was distributed in a 1928 Model T Ford to newsstands in Chester and in suburban Twin Oaks, Media, Sharon Hill, Darby and Chester Township. Joseph S. West and Charles Spain, two qualified teachers unable to land appropriate positions in the school system, served as circulation and advertising managers, respectively, in part because they recognized a need for such a publication, expressing hope it would succeed.

The editor was something of a throw-back to the uncompromising sheriff of the old West, armed, not with a six-shooter, but rather a pencil and pad, ready and anxious to take on the perpetrators of unjust deeds. His posse, in the beginning, consisted of a band of young vigilantes long waiting for a champion to lead them. Besides carrying hard news from reliable sources, the paper served as a sounding board by local individuals with knowledge or expertise in such fields as labor, social work, sports, entertainment, recreation, youth work, medical and veterans affairs. Some of the columnists were Alex Bouldin, Stan Jackson, Clifton Berry, Pecolia Floyd, Herman Laws, Catherine Durnell, Annie Green and Chauncey L. Campbell, a young able assistant editor.

In one more step to challenge the conservative leadership, a few of the "New Negro" faction stepped into the political waters for the November, 1945 city-wide elections. Their candidates, running as Democrats, included George T. Raymond for City Council; Wilson Harper, a young labor union agent, for School Board; and Norman "Jazz" Hunt, a former constable and brother of Joseph S. Hunt, for Ninth Ward Alderman. Political neophytes Raymond and Harper lost their bids, as did Hunt who once served his winning opponent Casper H. Green as a constable.

The *Crusader*, however, learned later that Raymond and his Democratic ticket had been subjected to some obvious trickery in months prior to the election. The three, having won their primaries, claimed they had been promised the votes of the Negro Independent Republicans in opposition to the McClure ticket, particularly precinct committeemen. Nothing like this ever happened. In fact, labor which ordinarily sided with Democrats offered only minimal support to the ticket, especially for Harper who happened to be one of their union brothers.[2]

Sometimes the *Crusader* and Blacks in general received unsolicited, though not too surprising, boosts in challenging segregation. At this particular time it was the case of Harry Mudrick, a pharmacist

Chapter 6

prescribing a healthy antidote for the owner of two jim-crow movie theaters, Matthew M. Margoline. Mudrick wrote in an open letter through the *Crusader*:

"Dear Sir: As a fellow Jew, I am appealing to you against further race discrimination which has been and still is being practiced in your theaters. Our race, persecuted for thousands of years, and not even with a national home of our own, should certainly be the last to discriminate because of race or religion.

"I trust your policies may change so that any decent citizen, upon paying admission, can take any seat in your theaters, and not be relegated to some balcony or special seat. I should hate to see something terrible like a race riot happen because of your policies. The Jew, because of your nationality, would certainly be blamed. That might happen because many of our darker brothers have seen colored as well as whites die for us ... and certainly will not stand for discrimination in their own home town. I will support my stand to the fullest extent even if it means taking legal steps to remedy this dirty situation."[3] Mudrick owned a pharmacy for many years at Ninth Street and Central.

It probably would have provided a more sensational spectacle for the Black community to follow a court case with Margoline facing charges of discrimination in a public place, a state law, and eventually paying a fine or going to jail. But the NAACP president, the *Crusader* editor and two other friends decided on the spur of the moment to give the Apollo Theater a personal rather than a legal test.

Having purchased tickets, the group marched themselves to seats in the middle rows of the movie house. But before they were comfortably seated, a young white usher rushed to them flashing a light in their faces, shouting excitedly, "You people can't sit here! No! No! You gotta take the last five rows you always have!" From out of the darkness, came an angry voice, obviously a white, telling the usher, "Shut up and git out my way. I can't see the picture." The harrassed usher left briefly, then returned with his boss Margoline.

Before the owner could say anything, Raymond asked him in a

NOTICE !
STOP   LOOK   AND READ

THE N. A. A. C. P.
wishes to report to the public business places who previously refused Negro patronage but now
HAVE CHANGED THEIR POLICY !
YOU CAN NOW BE SERVED
IN THE FOLLOWING PLACES

1. The Highway Diner, 9th & Lamokin St.
2. Shooster's Curb Service, 9th & Flower St.
3. Crystal Restaurant, 4th & Edgmont Ave.
4. Goff's, 8th & Edgmont Ave.
5. Circle, 3rd & Market St.

YOU CAN ALSO SIT ANYWHERE
IN THE FOLLOWING THEATRES

1. Strand Theatre, 3rd & Reaney
2. Apollo, 3rd & Lloyd
3. Washington, 4th & Market
4. Stanley, Fourth and Edgmont
5. State, 7th and Edgmont

If anyone is discriminated by any of the said business places or know of any business practicing discrimination please notify at once

George Raymond
1704 READING DRIVE   PHONE 2-6287

Watch for N.A.A.C.P. Bulletins for our next Mass Meeting.

NAACP flyer, announcing changes in segregation policies.

stern voice, "Do you want to meet us in court?" Without a reply, Margoline hastily retreated. The same group visited the Strand Theater a few nights later with only token opposition offered as they sat in the ground-floor seats rather than going to the "peanut gallery" where they had previously been relegated.[4]

Following its confrontations with the Margoline cinemas, the NAACP began questioning other businesses concerning their racial practices, eventually receiving affirmative confirmations from several establishments located in areas where Blacks either resided or went during shopping trips. As a result of the survey, the NAACP had fliers printed and distributed publicly with its message (see illustration).

Those were relatively small steps in attempts to ease the problems of public accommodations. Perhaps more insulting to the self-respect of hundreds of Black patrons were the persistent employment practices perpetuated by the Morris Mailman Dry Goods Store which had thrived for twenty-five years on West Third Street without ever hiring a single Black. When one *Crusader* board member, Dr. L. H. Hardy, presumed he would be more persuasive in soliciting advertisement than his young salesman, Mailman sent back the admonition that he would never purchase any advertisement for the paper as long as that "radical editor" was in charge. The editor, hoping to prove that Mailman was illustrating his anti-Black sentiment, inserted a sentence in the subsequent edition, reading, "R. E. Harris is no longer editor."[5] It was only a ruse. When Hardy returned later for the "promised" advertisement, he came away empty-handed. A few months later, however, and evidently due to the unfavorable publicity through stories in the *Crusader*, Mailman did place a small complimentary ad in the paper. Several months later, the store hired a female Black clerk.

For some unexplained reason, the scores of faithful patrons had tolerated the Mailman store fingering its nose at the community by tossing them a few cheap favors. A simple picket line harassing the establishment doubtlessly would have forced the owner to hire other capable Blacks from the growing jobless pool in the postwar period.

The Second Pew-McClure Bout

Frankly, the reform leaders simultaneously became deeply involved in what they considered two priority campaigns—one civic, the other political. They were launching an electrified school-improvement movement, and were being drawn into the second Pew-McClure political feud. The lingering matters of school inadequacies had finally come full circle in the forms of mass meetings, negotiations and picketings. The Pew factions, through their Black representatives, sought support by promising better considerations as their particular goals. To that extent, the Pew group purchased from the *Pittsburgh Courier* newspaper a series of articles to use as campaign literature. The articles, strongly critical of the McClure Black leaders in Chester and the community shortcomings they allowed to exist, had been written earlier by a local reporter.

The new Black Pew converts were even permitted to conceive and publish their own platform, though their only candidates on the ticket were precinct committee persons from the Eighth and Ninth Wards. The platform pledges were virtually the same objectives and goals civic groups had been seeking over the past decades. The candidates of U.S. Congress on both GOP tickets meant little or nothing to local voters. For instance, the Pew candidate E. Wallace Chadwick was a suburban corporate lawyer, and the McClure man was James Dewey, a former labor negotiator. Democrat Vernon O'Rourke, a young Swarthmore College professor, was the odd-man out, though he was the only candidate to publicly endorse the school campaign.

On that May, 1946 primary, politics did indeed make for some strange bedfellows. The Shipbuilders Union CIO agent Russ Watkins, who was using his sound-truck to aid the school fight, now led his union's endorsement of Dewey, McClure's candidate. Though Chadwick was unknown in Chester, he represented Pew, who hired Blacks only as common laborers prior to his lucrative contract from the federal government. Now that the war was over, would the Sun Shipyard revert to its old practices, many Blacks wanted to know.

When the city-county votes were tallied, Chadwick won over

Chapter 6

Dewey by less than 300 votes[6] yet in the city Black district all the McClure committee persons won—again. In some of those particular precincts, it was later revealed that less than half of the eligible voters bothered to go to the polls. Even some of those that did vote made it known they knew nothing of the principal candidates, and "cared not too much about the committeemen because they don't have the power to change anything," as one resident put it. One Negro Independent Republican poll-worker offered this assessment to the *Crusader* newspaper: "There, in my opinion, were three types of voters. One was looking for money to buy drinks. One gave in to the fastest talker. A third one voted for the side thought to be winning."[7]

Just prior to that 1946 primary, the National Urban League's Department of Research dispatched J. Harvey Kerns to conduct a survey of racial and socioeconomic conditions in Chester. Prior to his arrival, city authorities appointed its first Interracial Commission to cooperate in the study. While in town Kerns made only cursory visits to rank-and-file Black residents, whose reaction to the highly proclaimed "study" ranged from surprise to sarcasm. Most were aware that Kerns's committee was composed of individuals considered responsible for forging patterns of segregation or at least aiding in maintaining the system.

"It is imminently noticeable," editorialized the *Crusader*, "that some of the really liberal white citizens or some of the progressive-minded colored citizens were not among the Interracial Commission members." The final, full report seemed cloaked in secrecy, as no one among the reform leaders could recall seeing it. And the only finding released publicly were the recommendations for the appointments of interracial boards for certain social welfare agencies, including the Ruth L. Bennett Home, the Day Nursery and the Shelter for Colored Children, each of which were already amenable to interracial boards. The Colored Children's operations were sponsored by the Quakers and the Episcopal Church, both with a long history of liberal undertakings. Surprisingly, there was no mention in the public report concerning the deplorable housing situation. That may or may not have been an oversight. Two city Councilmen, Price and Kane, were also well-known realtors (for whom, coincidentally, streets in the all-white McCaffrey Housing project had been named).⁸

As to a complete report supposedly written by Mr. Kerns, none could ever be secured from the National Urban League headquarters.

Law Enforcement Lapses

The majority of the all-white City Council, part and parcel of a plot to line their pockets by peddling off the Chester Water Company, could hardly expect to show too much concern in ordering improvements in public safety for taxpayers despite the thriving wartime economy benefiting city coffers.

Clifford Peoples, the embarrassed mayor who resigned, innocent of the water company scandal boiling right under his nose, was succeeded by Ralph Swarts, whom McClure hand-picked for the vacancy. An ex-hardware store owner, Swarts did little to repair the fractured communication line between the progressive Black element and the machine. Once NAACP president George T. Raymond led a delegation to his honor's office to demand improvements in public safety, plus the addition of Black police. But Swarts, apparently sensitive to publicity lest he make statements tending to offend his political mentors, insisted that a Black reporter accompanying the group leave the room. "No, sir, he stays," Raymond countered sternly. It was realized by the group, who only wanted to put on public record their demands, that the mayor was not at liberty to offer any commitments.⁹

Numerous incidents of alleged brutality and civil rights denials by white law enforcement officials were being brought to the attention of the local NAACP. Although only a few of these accusations ever reached courtrooms, the association did succeed in securing freedom from jail for several Blacks who otherwise might have been railroaded.

One case eventually reaching the county courtroom in the winter of 1942 concerned two young Blacks being held responsible for the asphyxiation death of two white children. Daughters of a migrant worker residing in the William Penn Housing Project where Blacks were barred, the young victims were being cared for

Chapter 6

by a teen-aged Black girl with whom a 21-year-old boy friend had slept that night. The little girls' stepfather was also supposedly sleeping in another room at the time of the tragedy. The victims' mother, upon being notified of the deaths, rushed home from her graveyard shift before an ambulance could remove the bodies. She was reported crying to her husband, "Oh, Frank, why did you do it?" Nevertheless, the two Blacks were promptly arrested.

As usual, the NAACP began its own investigation, interviewing the detective handing the case. "How can you charge the young man with murder or manslaughter, and ignore the evidence that might point to the stepfather?" asked NAACP president Raymond. "Your report showed the father's room was next to the children's and the Black couple's was two doors away. How could gas from the range seep under the children's door without getting under the door of Frank's room which was next to the kitchen?"

"Well," the detective began thoughtfully, "there was a slight wind that blew the gas fumes right past the father's room. We think the boy himself turned on the gas.... As far as pressing charges against the parents for contributing to delinquency by allowing the colored boy to sleep there with a minor, we think they have suffered enough."

Despite the illogic of the bumbling investigation, a 9-count indictment was piled up against the young Black. However, when an assistant county prosecutor read the indictment preparatory to trial opening, Delaware County Judge Henry G. Sweney remarked wearily, "Throw out some of these charges! My Lord, you've got enough of them to sink a battleship!" The defendant, represented by Henry Gouley, whom the NAACP retained, was exonerated after a brief trial.[10]

The Independent Civic League again launched another campaign, this time for additional Black policemen, and the promotion of at least one to a detective position. Although the city's Black population was estimated at seventeen to twenty thousand, the organization contended that there was a need for more than the eight who primarily were assigned to south Chester in the wartime conditions. And specifically the ICL recommended Leroy Richardson and Oakley Berry, the youngest Blacks on the force to be promoted to detective status. Both men had recently earned certificates from a law enforcement school.[11] Shortly afterwards, however, the department made its own selection. Promoted as a Black patrolman was Theodore Laws, who had served as a police headquarters custodian for several years.

One of the popular veterans of the police department, Ellery Purnsley, later assigned to plain-clothes duty, met a tragic death in early 1948 on lower Market Street near his residence. A young war veteran being cheated out of his "numbers" or policy winnings went on a shooting rampage, killing Purnsley and eight other pedestrians in what was termed the "Market Street Massacre."[12] The area was the infamous "Bethel Court."

In theory, the Police Department could be indirectly blamed for the death of Purnsley and the other victims in the slaughter that occurred a few blocks from its headquarters. Had the law enforcement authorities broken up or curtailed the widespread illicit policy gambling, it might not have exploded. The racket which flourished for years particularly in Black neighborhoods doubtlessly enjoyed protection from some higher-up authorities—a fact to be proven more than once in the coming years.

First School Campaign Launched

"How can you expect to have a progressive city when you help breed ill-feelings between white and Black children by giving the whites good schools and designating deplorable and rotten facilities for Black children. We come here tonight peacefully. Perhaps the next generation appearing here and asking for decent schools will not come so peacefully!" Thus clearly and forcefully spoke Angela McLinn, wife of a dentist, Harry, who served in the U.S. 92nd Division overseas.

"Angie," a cream-colored young expectant mother, considered herself speaking for all Chester's Blacks, once more begging the Board of Education to improve buildings attended by their children, and to allow others to attend facilities nearest their homes. The five board members listened, on this May 21, 1946, somewhat perplexedly. This sort of talk from those folks had never been heard by the all-white body. Committees coming before

Chapter 6

them in the previous years were usually headed by clergymen and composed of polite mothers and a few docile fathers. Bristling with indignation and honestly puzzled by the defiant attitude of the group, Frank Andrews, board president and a bank official, drummed nervously on the shiny conference table. A part-time politician, he had also dealt tolerantly with "good colored folks" negotiating home mortgages or helping those seeking teaching jobs. Thoughtfully, he sized up this latest delegation. Besides Mrs. McLinn were Cecil Bond, an ex-high school basketball star and his wife, Frinjella, president of the Watts School Mothers Club; Ethel Brown, its secretary; George T. Raymond, president of the local NAACP branch; and numerous other citizens, all parents still smarting from the humiliating aftereffects of inferior school facilities, particularly Watts Elementary School.

"They still are only Negroes," Andrews apparently reasoned to himself. Furthermore, aside from being board spokesman, he doubtlessly heeded the voice from the eighth floor of the Crozer building, where "boss" McClure was located. So he reverted once more to the stereotyped reply to such delegations: "The matter will be taken under consideration."[13]

Although the board members may not have realized it, Andrew's curt reply was the signal for what would ultimately become a full-scale campaign against the entire school system, and consequently the political machine as well. Had not the Mothers Club sponsored an "open house" for taxpayers to observe firsthand the unsanitary and unsafe conditions at Watts, the campaign may not have gained the swift momentum it did. The basement toilets were putrid-smelling. There were holes in walls that had loose plastering. Some windows had no curtains. The teachers' room was a small closet with a crude stretcher made of wood and sackcloth. Most alarming was that the 56-year-old school with an enrollment of over four hundred students lacked a fire escape.[14]

The morning following the meeting at the school board, parents supported by growing crowds began rounds of picketing at Watts, the school administration building, and briefly the residence of the Rev. D. A. Scott, the interim school board member succeeding L. M. Hunt. They circulated petitions, sponsored mass meetings, wrote the state board of education and contacted the local health authorities, seeking school reforms and improvements. The Mothers Club was soon joined by the Home-School Association, the NAACP, the Independent Civic League, the Progressive Men's Club and the Fairgrounds Residents Council of Chester Township, whose members' children always transferred to Chester Junior High classes.

This public-spirited consortium soon broadened its goals to include improvements in law enforcement, street lighting and sewers, housing, public transportation and the elimination of segregation in all schools and public places. The political bosses, naturally, were resisting these efforts in every manner at their disposal, except overt violence. Yet the in midst of the fray, an interesting yet contradictory message was heard from the person who was the first to open his church doors for mass meetings. The Rev. J. Pius Barbour, pastor of Calvary Baptist Church, dispatched an "open letter" to the *Crusader* addressed specifically to the "Young Folks." (The campaign leaders were all in the 25-year-age bracket.)

Classifying himself as an "Elder Statesman," Barbour wrote, "My job is to stand on the sideline, cheer and give advice." Contrasting the civil rights tactics of gradualism and direct action, he advised young people to pursue long-range goals instead of direct action. "You can't clean up the school system, tear down all bad housing, get enough policemen, close jim-crow theaters," he continued, "you can't get new buses, new sewers, better street lighting all the same time. DROP EVERYTHING BUT THE SCHOOL FIGHT!"[15]

By this time, however, at least the school campaign seemed well on its way to a relative resolution because, after all, state laws were being violated. Yet had Barbour, who maintained friendly relations with local politicos, acquired some inside hint of possible physical peril to the young reform leaders bent on derailing the political machine in their bailiwick? No matter, the organization planned to carry out the campaign beyond the ramifications of the political machine.

Unfortunately, there were no Black attorneys in Chester; and despite the efforts of a few in the reform group to retain a white counselor, Henry Gouley, who previously handled a few cases involving Black clients, a majority swung a decision to preferably seek a "Philadelphia lawyer." At one suggestion, organization leaders contacted the Educational Equality League of Philadelphia. Since its founding in 1932, it had fought and won school cases on its home grounds as well as in suburban areas.[16] Its membership included such prominent legal minds as Floyd Logan, president; John Francis Williams; Rufus Watson; and E. Washington Rhodes, *Philadelphia Tribune* publisher and a former state legislator.

The attorneys advised parents to attempt to enroll their children in schools nearest their homes. As expected, practically all the pupils were refused enrollment in those schools, including Dewey-Mann, several blocks from Watts, Franklin Street School and Smedley Junior High, which students had to pass en route to Douglass Junior High, approximately seven miles farther. The white principals involved claimed either that the transfers were not properly completed or that school superintendent F. Herman Fritz ordered them to refuse to accept the transfers. Fritz announced the board would make a decision on the issue "by next September."

Meanwhile, authorities were still promising to repair Watts, but parents insisted on an entirely new structure. During a mass meeting in mid-June, 1946 at St. Daniel's Methodist Church, Educational Equality League leaders addressed an overflowing gathering. Joseph H. Rainey, the hard-driving president of the Philadelphia NAACP, one of the speakers, criticized the "hankerchief-head Uncle Toms for allowing such a damnable situation to exist." Asking the whereabouts of the Black member of the school board, and learning Rev. D. A. Scott, the recently appointed member, was not present, Rainey urged that his home be picketed. "I'll even come down tomorrow to help picket, if you want me," he shouted.[17]

"KEEP NIGGERS OUT!" was splashed in white paint on the Franklin School located on the edge of a racially mixed neighborhood, yet designated for whites only. This was one of the schools where parents, on advice of their attorneys, were sending their children who were regularly rejected by the principals. In apparent connection with the warning, *Crusader* board member Dr. L. M. Hardy told of seeing a note sent to the Main YMCA office indicating that the Ku Klux Klan was helping back opposition to integrated schools. (Incidentally, no public hint of KKK activities in the town had been heard of for years, nor would any be in the immediate future.) "We don't want to be responsible for any trouble in this town," he admonished, referring to the editor's strong involvement in the school controversy.

School Hires Two *Crusader* Owners

Rather surprisingly, a few weeks later Hardy revealed that he and fellow-board member Dr. W. H. Henderson were appointed by school authorities to positions examining the dental and physical well-being of Black pupils. Were these tokens from the powers-that-be one more ploy to curtail operations of the reform movement's principal means of communication? Through the simplest of interpretations, this paradoxical move spelled a flagrant conflict of interest for the two, based on the *Crusader's* viable role in the anti-discrimination campaign. Both men, presumably as self-sufficient financially as any other Black professional in town, obviously demonstrated their willingness to switch their allegiance to the political bosses rather than fully support the pursuance of an ideal beneficial to Black citizens who supported them 100 percent as patients. Hardy, moreover, had been secretly conducting a search for someone to replace the editor, whether or not he could guarantee a majority of the votes of six board members to effect such an ouster.

When authorities found themselves unable to break the school strike, they announced that the strike-absented pupils would not be able to get their report cards, and consequently would be flunked. In response, teachers passed out report cards on school grounds just prior to the semester's end. The next step by authorities was to charge Watts parents with truancy for keeping the approximately four hundred pupils from classes. The parents willingly appeared before Alderman Holton and were fined $20 each. Frinjella Bond, Watts Mothers Club president, for instance, was fined $100 for keeping her five sons home. However, all the fines were guaranteed by former school board member Lewis M.

Chapter 6

Frinjella Bond-Watson (left) and Anna Hollingsworth, in 1989, discuss their experiences in the 1946 school integration movement.

Hunt and Jack Farrell, Moonglow Cafe owner.

All the cases were appealed and scheduled to be heard in mid-September at the Delaware County Common Pleas Court in Media, the county seat. Mrs. Ethel Brown, the Mothers Club secretary, had the privilege of delivering the subpoena to school board president Frank G. Andrews at his bank office. "His face turned so red," she recalled." I didn't know if he was surprised, mad or what, but I didn't care a bit. I felt good that we were going to have our day in court."

Educational Equality League attorneys John Francis Williams and Rufus Watson, handling the case, gratis, presented arguments to judge Henry G. Sweney who without hesitation ordered the school board to obey the Pennsylvania state laws which decreed that no child should pass one school to attend another because of race or color. He further ruled that no pupils should enter Watts School building until all necessary renovations were completed in order to make it safe and sanitary.

Four of the persistent mothers, Mesdames Bond, Brown, Wilma Simpson and Anna Hollingsworth, recalled their responses to the long-awaited court ruling. One said, "We walked out of the courtroom in a quiet, dignified manner; but soon as we boarded the bus, we let out loud shouts of joy!"[18]

Thus the school campaign was relatively successful in reaching the goals of Black civic organizations. Watts was quickly renovated and other students enrolled in classes nearest their homes,

Politics and Prejudice

including Smedley Junior High in the Seventeenth Street area where the ancient two-room George Jones School was demolished. On the downside, there was no integration of teachers, as that issue was not approached by campaign leaders. Douglass Junior High continued housing ninth grade Black students, classes which ordinarily would be the responsibility of Chester High. All in all, many community leaders felt fairly good about their small successes and no doubt would eventually push further for broader goals.

Through hindsight, it could easily be assumed that the political rejection of James H. Grasty as the Douglass School principal was a highly probable factor more than indirectly responsible for the mild revolution not only leading to the first step in the school integration campaign, but also to the beginnings of positive changes in other phases of life in the Black community. Had not Grasty cooperated, indeed often encouraged the Watts mothers, the entire reform activities may not have been so easily and effectively launched. Other school principals in the past seldom subscribed to the idea of tax-paying parents involving themselves in "their" schools. Grasty, an independent-minded educator entering his twentieth year in the local school system, always stressed a strong obligation to the community in which he and his

Left: William Grasty. Right: Edward Grasty.

Chapter 6

family long resided. One brother, William, was the city's first U.S. Postman; and another, Edward, was also a schoolteacher.

The *Crusader* editor, seeing several of the paper's aims realized or at least pointed on the road to accomplishments, resigned to accept another journalist post out of town. The *Crusader*, the first paper with local ownership had been fairly well received by advertisers and readers of both races. It closed down shortly after the editor left.

Nearing the end of the twentieth century's first half, the Black population in Chester had reached an estimated 35 percent. Blacks also accounted for a total 45 percent in Chester Township from where numerous residents had been drawn during the war. Those particular families, except for voting privileges there, did most of their shopping and socializing in Chester; and by special arrangements among authorities, their children entered the seventh grades in Chester schools.

Thanks largely to the rise and development of grass-roots movements after three years of intense struggles, Chester Blacks were beginning slowly to rise to grounds equal to those of more fortunate citizens. Still, they needed to adopt new techniques and to follow the expertise offered by newfound allies in order to prepare for the long haul. Two crucially important movements, the YMCA and school reform campaigns, both youth-aimed, had each molded into organizations functioning fairly successfully. This was despite differences in ages, politics, socioeconomics or church affiliations—factors oftentimes interfering in other undertakings—not necessarily just by Blacks.

Equally significant were the school reform activities almost dovetailing in time with the YMCA drive, which, however, operated in a much shorter period of precise planning and execution. On the other hand, the school campaign represented day-by-day, long drawn-out maneuvers, dominated by mothers whose concerns were much more personal and intimate. The females, moreover, capitalized on the strong awareness by their neighbors of their common problems, having developed a warm rapport among themselves over the years. Their relations were unlike many in the YMCA campaign, where some of the participants were newcomers, or were people had never become acquainted with others, mainly due to social or economic differences (real or imagined). The "Y" movement, furthermore, depended upon a sizable number of professionals or college-trained participants who generally were able to control their schedules, while the fathers of school children were seldom able to join their wives on the picket lines or at meetings because of their daily laborers' jobs.

When "Dick" Thomas, the Wharton School product, appealed for "oneness of purpose" among Blacks during the climax of the "Y" drive, he added, "We can be the controlling power in the city." Unfortunately, he did not see two years hence when women began taking on the political machine on behalf of their most important cause. Such a combination of leadership—progressive males and females—representing over a fourth of the city's population might possibly have accomplished much more in civic reforms. If not nearly enough reforms were realized, indeed, it must be remembered that this 1943-47 period preceded the nationwide civil rights revolution by a whole generation.

How many of the four-hundred-some Watts School long-suffering pupils and the children of the YMCA adherents would remember and represent future citizens and taxpayers in the 1960s and beyond?

POSTWAR ERA SPARKS CIVIC AWAKENING
Bibliography

1. *Crusader* newspaper, Vol. 1, No. 1.

2. Ibid, November 10, 1945.

3. Ibid, May 18, 1946.

4. Ibid, June 3, 1946.

5. Ibid, August 9, 1946.

6. Ibid, May 24, 1946.

7. Ibid, May 24, 1946.

8. R. E. Harris, *Delinquency In Our Democracy* (Philadelphia: Wetzel

Publishing, 1954), p. 33.

9. *Crusader*, March 21, 1946.

10. Harris, *Delinquency*, p. 32.

11. *Crusader*, June 3, 1946.

12. *Chester Times*, November 6, 1948.

13. Harris, *Delinquency*, pp. 19-20.

14. *Crusader*, May 18, 1946.

15. Ibid, July 12, 1946.

16. V. P. Franklin, *The Education of Black Philadelphia* (University of Pennsylvania Press, 1979), pp. 137-39. Also *Philadelphia Tribune* newspaper, March 24, 1932.

17. *Crusader*, June 15, 1946.

18. Interviews with author, May 1989.

Chapter 7

Town Undergoes Strange Metamorphosis (1951-60)

BLACK RESIDENTS INCREASE SUBSTANTIALLY; WHITES FLEE TO SUBURBS

Chester was on the verge of a complete metamorphosis during the beginning of the last half of the twentieth century as the winding down of the war efforts began to be felt by virtually every facet of the city. Some changes were relatively positive, others definitely negative. White flight to the county started in earnest while Black in-migrations came in leaps and bounds. White population in the 1950-60 decade decreased by approximately 10,000, while Blacks increased by 7,000 for a total of 21,000, making a 54 percent jump in the decade. Moreover, considered beneficial to the city in general was the arrival of scores of Black professionals—physicians, dentists, attorneys and teachers—obviously recognizing the-growing potential for their services. Some willingly took on added responsibilities as community activists.

On the surface, improvements in the civil rights area might be observed through the appearances of young Blacks for the first time working as bank tellers or retail store clerks in the business district. Public accommodations were open to all, though movie theaters and restaurants in that section were closing or relocating to the county. At any rate, young Blacks could enjoy recreation and social events at the West End Branch YMCA, finally constructed in South Chester after years of waiting, or at the new Central YMCA or the YWCA, both now fully integrated. In face of the growing unemployment picture, such free pastime activities were godsends to many youths and adolescents.

"Don't be fooled," warned George T. Raymond, NAACP president since 1943, "all that glitters is not gold. It's a constant battle. We can't let down our guards for an instant." He was speaking to a former resident on a visit. He pointed out that there still was no true school integration, despite the anti-segregation movement he helped to spearhead. "Some coloreds," he continued using his reference to the race, "are attending schools nearest to their

Chapter 7

George Raymond

homes, but teachers are not integrated. Pretty soon we're going to have all colored schools once more if some action isn't taken."[1]

Even though Blacks now comprised 40 percent of Chester High School students, all the faculty and administration was white. Many Black parents therefore were expressing keen disappointment with the lack of practical counseling offered their children under this situation. Charles Swiggett, who showed very little outward interest in these matters in the war years, was now concerned about a son who had entered the high school. "Sure, we have lots of colored kinds coming out of there," he said, going on to criticize what he termed "production-line" education. "They get bad counseling and guidance," he continued. "It's discriminatory in the worst way. I know kids who've been steered away from curriculums that probably prepare them adequately for future careers. Sometimes I think it would be better for a kid to quit and train elsewhere for the vocation he likes rather than being trained inadequately."[2]

In spite of all the dissatisfaction that had been loudly voiced by the Black community about the inferior buildings attended by their children, none except the George Jones School had been closed since the court case of 1946. Instead, as Raymond pointed out, Black pupils were permitted to attend the previously "all-white" buildings nearest their residences. But now with new families moving into the neighborhoods, some of these buildings were literally bursting at the seams by overcrowding, especially in the cases of the slightly improved Watts building, plus Dewey-

Mann and Franklin, the latter two located in areas surrounded by Blacks. Portable classrooms, moreover, were necessary to handle the increased pupil load at Booker T. Washington School.

As many of the old-line Black teachers reached retirement, they were replaced by many more instructors necessary to handle increased student loads. This situation evidently took the wind out of some of the usual politics used in the selection of teachers. For example, two highly respected, qualified teachers, Charles Spain and Joseph S. West, who had been passed over for years by the political system, finally received appointments. Spain, a Cheyney alumnus, succeeded James H. Grasty as Watts principal and was later reassigned to Franklin, then eventually to an administrative post at Chester High. West, a product of West Chester Teachers College and a pillar of the community, taught at Douglass until his retirement. John Driggins was the last principal at Watts, which would be finally demolished after seventy years of heavy usage.

For those Blacks fortunate enough to graduate from high school with academic or vocational courses of their choosing, opportunities for furtherance of their training were generally within walking or busing distance. At one time, college students had to reside on out-of-town campuses. Eventually, their options would include Penn Morton (later Widener University), Swarthmore College, West Chester State, and local branches of Delaware County Community College. Most of the institutions sponsored Black Student Unions or Centers. Widener, located on the grounds of the old Pennsylvania Military College, has at times had as many as an estimated 10 percent Blacks. Its president, Dr. Clarence R. Moll, would go on to be a leading force in future civil rights movements. The once highly selective Swarthmore College has had an estimated 8 percent Black students among its 1,200.

Law Enforcement Scandal Erupts

It wasn't long after the senseless tragedy of the "Market Street Massacre" (with a frustrated numbers player shooting to death policeman Ellery Purnsley and eight other citizens—see Chapter 6) when a gambling investigation reached Chester and indirectly resulted in the downfall of Deputy Sheriff Albert Reading. In fact, it appeared that Reading was being "thrown to the wolves" for

Chapter 7

being accused of the type of lawbreaking generally suspected as accepted practice among those who enjoyed close relations with the political machine.

Crime-busting Philadelphia District Attorney Richardson Dilworth, during his investigations, came upon a trail that led from his city to Chester. A Chester bag man for a Philadelphia and Delaware County numbers operator claimed he paid Reading $50 weekly for a guarantee that gambling could operate unmolested in Chester.[3] Then, from the Media county jail a female prisoner told Judge Henry G. Sweney in December, 1952, that Reading had earlier solicited $600 from her, promising he would persuade Judge Sweney to reduce her sentence for shoplifting. By this time, Reading was obviously becoming an embarrassment to certain authorities; and through some mysterious manipulations, he was allowed to draw down his $3,200 pension in October, 1953, and quickly disappear from Chester, even unbeknownst to his wife who was attending a funeral at the time.[4]

While the alleged corruption controversies surrounding Reading were spreading, the biggest wholesale shake-up in the Chester Police Department occurred "because of failure to clean up vice and other unsavory conditions." This surprise move came when it was thought by some that officials feared the rackets spotlights were swinging to the police operations. In the house-cleaning moves, the chief of police and two captains were forced into retirement; two other captains, five sergeants and eight detectives were reduced to the ranks of patrolmen.[5]

Public explanation of the action came from assistant Director of Public Affairs Francis X. Kelly, a former sergeant in the State Police Barracks in Media, who stated, "It has come to my attention that some policemen have seen vice and have chosen to ignore it. I know through personal investigations that there are numbers being played, bookies operating, prostitution going on and marijuana being sold." Kelly furthermore disbanded the two-man vice squad and added, "Each man from now on is on his own. He can get back his rank or promotion strictly on the basis of merit and when the city is cleaned up."[6] The one Black caught in the shake-up was Detective Theodore Laws, a former department custodian promoted to rookie status a few years earlier when Blacks pushed for equal opportunities in the bureau.

A short time later when Kelly was asked if any further investigation of the department was going on, he replied succinctly, "No. The man who was implicated was gotten rid of,"[7] presumably referring to Reading, although he failed to explain the reasons for the forced retirement of the Chester police chief and two captains.

In the meantime, while Reading was still missing, Delaware County District Attorney Raymond R. Start wrote Dilworth seeking any investigative information he possessed concerning Delaware County. The Philadelphia official refused, blasting the request in a letter:

"The activities of the recently resigned deputy sheriff were known to every policeman in the county and must have been known by law enforcement agencies in Chester. It was common knowledge even in Philadelphia that if you wanted to engage in numbers or horse-racing business in Chester you had to see Reading who acted as representative in the transaction.

"It is strange that the sheriff and law enforcement of the city would permit Reading to resign suddenly, withdraw his pension and vanish. It said, in effect 'Get out of here! Take your money with you and keep your mouth shut or we will make you the goat!' No effort has been made to locate Reading and bring about his return."[8]

In October, 1953, a warrant was issued for the arrest of the missing ex-deputy sheriff, charging him with "extortion, bribery, corrupt solicitation and malfeasance." A month later, Delaware County Judge Van Roden, on vacation in the West, reported that he spotted Reading being driven by a woman in a Pennsylvania-licensed car near Gallup, New Mexico. But upon checking fugitive records at the police headquarters, he could find no record pertaining to Reading.[9] A month or so later, however, Reading returned and surrendered to the courts. Lewis M. Hunt, Chester undertaker and Black GOP leader, posted a $500 bail for him.[10]

At his trial in April, 1954, Reading, whose personal relations with John J. McClure extended thirty years back, was sentenced

Chapter 7

to six months in jail and fined $2,000 on charges of bribery and extortion. "I never got a penny from the case," he protested in his defense, "the jury found me guilty and I am willing to put myself in God's hands and in the mercy of the court." Dr. Lancess McKnight told the court Reading was suffering from high blood pressure and multiple arthritis and would not survive his sentence. But Judge Sweney, whose reputation as a straight-shooting and independent jurist had obviously been besmirched by Reading's falsely involving him in the deal with the female prisoner, simply replied, "We are sorry, but the jury has spoken."[11]

Upon his release from jail, the 65-year-old one-time political dynamo appeared a broken man, physically and spiritually. He did not live long afterwards—a sad commentary on a flamboyant man that white politicians depended on immensely to sing their praises among his people.

The troubled police department was soon to have its field of operations reduced slightly, according to the city Redevelopment Authority. The Bethel Court section, located a mere shouting distance from the department, would be completely razed to make room for a Scott Paper Company parking facility.

"The area is known to past and present generations mostly for its wickedness," a columnist for the *Evening Bulletin* wrote in an over-simplification of the situation, "a real hot spot where vice flourished and whose name was whispered in most ports of call on the seven seas, carried by word of mouth by seamen who also knew such ports as Singapore and Suez."[12]

No doubt, with mixed feelings, some of the 400 families would be relocated. Fortunately, most would be settled in the Ruth L. Bennett Terrace Homes, a low-cost housing project being completed in south Chester by the local Housing Authority.[13] Such significant landmarks as the Robert Wade Neighborhood House, the Welsh Street AME Church and the Moonglow Hotel and Cafe had to be demolished in the name of "progress."

County Against Black Residents

White families began fleeing to county environs for various reasons, especially the rapidly shrinking job market and their resentment at the integration movement. But when some Blacks who supported and even helped lead the civil rights battles attempted to seek adequate housing in some county neighborhoods, the opposition of whites proved far more vitriolic than that experienced from previous antagonists in Chester. Two such cases were significant.

George Raymond and Wilson Harper, two young men helping spark the 1946 integration activities, had to literally fight for their lives when they sought to exercise their rights to seek more comfortable lives for their families in "all-white" communities in separate parts of Delaware County.

Raymond and his family had resided in Lamokin Village housing project while he was ramrodding the school integration campaign. Soon he would attempt to seek a more permanent home for his wife and young children outside the city, totally unaware he would be entering the most crucial battle of his activist career. A few Blacks were moving out of their communities, where homes had deteriorated badly from a half-century of heavy usage and neglect, and into neighboring areas. Even fewer families, those financially better off, were purchasing homes in Upper Chichester and Chester Township, both located adjacent to Chester. Raymond, employed as a janitor at Scott Paper Company, decided to negotiate to purchase a home in the borough of Rutledge, five miles northeast of the town. "I knew Eddystone, Ridley Park or Clifton Heights were for whites only, but I didn't know about

House-warming event by George Raymond (left) after winning legal battle for occupancy. Those attending included the Rev. F. D. Jones, William Raymond, L. Brown, NAACP and Quaker supporters.

Chapter 7

Rutledge," he later admitted in 1956 upon realizing the extreme difficulty he was undergoing. He and his wife, Iola, had bid on an 108-year-old 3-bedroom house, having been encouraged by a Quaker-owned realty firm dedicated to the fair housing principal in the county.

The family was ready to move into the house when a mysterious fire originating in the basement gutted the interior and burned off part of the roof. Raymond suspected arson, but state investigators determined that was not the case. More complications arose when town officials denied him a permit to rebuild, deciding the property should be condemned. Displaying his usual determination, Raymond decided to seek legal relief—one of his attorneys being Robert A. Wright, a boyhood friend recently out of law school. Eventually, the Common Pleas Court overturned the building inspector's ruling, granting Raymond the right to rebuild his home.

Thus, after a two-year delay, the Raymonds were ready to take occupancy of their home—this renovated building in the town of less than 1,000 white families. He would make it an important occasion, a house-warming attended by businessmen, clergymen and Quaker friends who supported his long-suffering efforts.

By no stretch of the imagination, however, were the Raymonds' troubles behind them. Having disposed of opposition from town authorities, the family now had to contend with some bigoted townspeople who finally came to the realization that they had an unwanted family in their midst. Some of these folks, observing the Raymonds originally inspecting the property in company with a white female real estate agent, were obviously under the impression the Blacks were servants of the white woman inspecting the property for possible purchase. Shortly after settling down in their home, someone set fire to Halloween cornstalks decorating their entrance-way. At another time, wife Iola was forced to fire a shotgun from the upstairs window to scare off someone taking potshots at their property. The harassment tactics were even lowered to one of the Raymonds' grandchildren, who complained that some white children were telling other elementary school pupils not to play with her because she was Black. A left-handed

Politics and Prejudice

Wilson Harper, and the union office building named in his honor.

comment about the Raymonds was supposedly made by a right-leaning resident: "These people are not as bad as you thought they were," he remarked, "I found out that all Black people aren't niggers."[14]

Harper, an officer in both the local NAACP and the Independent Civic League, was also business agent for Local 413 Laborers Union. A 1933 graduate of Chester High School, he was the first Black to become a union officer in the county. In 1958 he decided to become the first of his race to purchase a home in Drexel Hill. First came weekend harassments which he wanted to attribute to mere youth pranks; yet with such incidents as attempted fire-bombing and the tossing of two-by-four boards through his window, Harper sought help from the Upper Darby Police Department, whose jurisdiction included Drexel Hill.

"One night," he recalled, "I noticed an unmarked police car parked nearby and assumed it was there to provide my security; but when my house was attacked again, the car left immediately. Realizing we could get no help from the local law enforcement, I decided to take my complaints to the State Police."

So after enduring the problems for six months, thanks to the State Police, Harper's troubles ceased. He noted that a Jewish woman had been his most reliable supporter during his ordeal. He was later elected administrator of the Health and Welfare Fund of his union, the five-county District Council of Building Construction, serving for twenty-five years until his retirement.[15]

Chapter 7

Black Churches Increase, Serve Community

Many of those families fortunate enough to acquire homes in various parts of the county seldom severed their memberships in their Chester church congregations, where some had served since early childhood. Like some of their long-time members, more than a few of the old-line Black churches purchased and occupied edifices abandoned by white churches that followed their members out of town. Most of these sturdily built but ancient buildings were located either on West Seventh Street, halfway between the Black and former white neighborhoods, or on West Third Street between Jeffrey Street and Highland Avenue.

An interesting illustration of the old and new in the local pursuit of religious activities could be seen at Third and Jeffrey Streets where catercornered from one another were the recently organized Community United Methodist Church and the Spencer Union African Methodist Episcopal Church. The latter was organized in 1845 as the first Black congregation in Chester, then known as the Welsh Street Union AME. Its new name was in tribute to the denomination's founder, Peter Spencer. Noteworthy, too, was Rev. Spencer's inauguration of the "August Quarterly," an annual day-long Sunday religious ecumenical celebration in Wilmington, Delaware, drawing crowds from Maryland, Delaware and Pennsylvania.

St. John's African Union Methodist Protestant Church moved from its Seventeenth and Walnut Street location to Seventh Street and Lincoln, making way for the Widener College campus. The Range's Temple Church of God in Christ constructed its third edifice at Seventh and Fulton Streets, having sold its Second Street and Central Avenue structure. The other large First Pentecostal Holiness Church bought the Knights of Columbus building on Pusey near West Third Street.

A few congregations built new quarters in the Black community. Shiloh Baptist Church, formerly at Ninth Street and Tilghman, constructed its new edifice at Seventh Street and Central Avenue, long-time site of the controversial tavern owned by white GOP leader Ed Fry. Murphy AME Church abandoned its old building on lower Townsend Street and built anew at Seventh and Yarnall

Politics and Prejudice

One of the numerous storefront churches along West Third Street.

Streets.

Other prominent congregations held to their original locations, expanding programs and services beneficial to their surrounding neighborhoods. This category includes St. Daniel's United Methodist, Calvary and Providence Baptist, St. Luke's Christian Methodist and Thomas M. Thomas Presbyterian (formerly "Fifth" Presbyterian). Individually, these churches acquired surrounding properties where substandard or deteriorating buildings were cleared away to be utilized for recreation or parking spaces for members. St. Luke's congregation relocated across the street to the remodeled former Benn Theater, yet still retained use of its original building.

Members and friends of St. Daniel's United Methodist Church attended its annual Father and Sons Banquet June 12, 1971.

Chapter 7

Store-front churches—"missions" or "Temples" as some preferred to be known—spread, sometimes two to a single block, along West Third Street to Highland Avenue. They mostly occupied former sites of once-successful small business-places. Predominantly of the pentecostal or "holiness" bent, these churches appealed generally to the middle-aged or elderly, lately from the rural south. Not many of these congregations became involved in social or community issues.

TOWN UNDERGOES STRANGE METAMORPHOSIS
Bibliography

1. Interview with Raymond by the author.

2. Interview with Swiggett by the author.

3. *Philadelphia Evening Bulletin*, October 25, 1953.

4. *Philadelphia Inquirer*, October 25, 1953.

5. *Chester Times*, May 26, 1953.

6. Ibid.

7. Ibid, May 30, 1953.

8. *Inquirer*, October 25, 1953.

9. Ibid, November 7, 1953.

10. *Evening Bulletin*, January 27, 1954.

11. *Inquirer*, April 10, 1954.

12. *Evening Bulletin*, January 13, 1953.

13. *Chester Times*, August 20, 1954.

14. Interview with Raymond.

15. Interview with Harper.

Chapter 8

New Black Leadership Cadre Emerges (1961-70)

HUNDREDS BEATEN, JAILED BEFORE SCHOOL INTEGRATION WINS IN COURT

Moving into the sixties, the city saw a new breed of leadership beginning to emerge and assert itself among Blacks, not just in politics, but among the professionals and, grass-roots activists as well. Most of the old professional class generally stayed on the sidelines while still earning their daily bread from many of those fighting for fair treatment. Now, young professionals and their newcomer constituents were stepping in front of the pack. A few of the old-line Black political leaders, upon seeing the parade for progress passing them by, stepped feebly in line for one last hurrah, reluctantly aligning themselves with such organizations as the NAACP whose leaders they once considered too "radical."

Meanwhile, up-and-coming young Black political neophytes (in sharp contrast to the disappearing GOP henchmen who had to fend financially for themselves while their bosses profited royally) assumed fairly equal footing with the white bosses, whether or not their deals were shady or illegal. They had indeed learned well from the "masters."

The aging McClure, who would die in 1965,[1] and his succeeding "War Board," was obviously aware of the rapid increase in the Black potential power as well as the sharp decrease among its white political base, and accepted this reality in the scheme of things. Consequently, instead of risking chances of their favored Black not winning at the polls against a popular Democrat or an independent, the powers-that-be, after a well-timed resignation of the incumbent, would appoint someone of their choosing to fill the vacancy. This type of maneuver most definitely was guaranteed to carry him or her safely through subsequent elections. Upon winning a permanent seat, some of them were often made party to games of musical chairs—or to be more mundane—chess, with its Black knights, queens, bishops and rooks being constantly shifted around.

Chapter 8

Unlike in past years, however, there were now no absolute assurances that all of the chosen young-bloods would stay quietly in the niches carefully chosen for them. Even in the police department, which periodically showed evidences of corruption and inefficiency, a few young rookies often posed outright, embarrassing challenges to the king-makers. A young Black sergeant, for instance, who also happened to be an ordained preacher and a former NAACP officer, revealed publicly that he had rejected a promotion being arranged by a policy boss through a superior officer. At another time, an ex-lieutenant, related by marriage to the politically powerful Richardson, attempted to run for the office of mayor, even after heading the reform-minded Black policemen's organization. More evidence of similar incidents would surface in the near future.

A few years after his personal housing victory in Rutledge, long-time NAACP president George T. Raymond was to have plenty of live bodies in his sometimes lonely campaigns against injustices and neglect towards his race. Next to joblessness, that reached a serious state among Blacks, was the festering, recurring problem of school inequality. Widespread unemployment, while inconveniencing many, did have one beneficial effect: the involuntarily idle diverted much of their anger towards the one issue that appeared vulnerable in the armor of the city political machine—school segregation. Under such circumstances, former grassroots activists and their baby-boomer offspring were apparently chomping at the bit to launch another challenge.

In a sense, an appreciable number of Chester rank-and-file Blacks were at last coming of age. Over their television sets and radios, this generation was doubtlessly gaining broad and knowledgeable appreciation of the civil rights tactics and strategies utilized by participants in the Black Revolution spreading across the nation. Many young Blacks must have viewed and listened to their role models in the likes of the fearless leaders who risked jail, police dogs, nightstick beatings and even death for their marches. The Rev. Martin Luther King, whom some remembered as the assistant pastor at Calvary Baptist Church, stood tallest among the national crusaders.

Politics and Prejudice

Moreover, few of the younger residents were aware or even cared about local political ramifications certain to threaten any intransigence among residents. But they were seriously in need of a strong, nervy and untrammeled champion who could devote full time to their cause. Luckily, into this breach soon jumped a former Army paratrooper who earned his spurs in the Korean conflict. Stanley E. Branche would be the daring generalissimo to take charge of the sputtering campaign. Raymond, a few hometown lawyers, and the NAACP regional director, reluctant at first to join ranks with the flamboyant, militant Branche, finally did. They soon formed a leadership cadre that drew hundreds of the city's impatient Blacks for what turned out to be a long, bitter conflict.

New Black Champion Leads

Branche came to town in early 1962, having married the former Anna Layton, a stepdaughter of "Daddy" Bass, a McClure lackey.[2] An impassioned speaker, he reminded his followers, particularly newcomers, that they were being deprived of their rights by the McClure faction. At mass meetings in churches and on street corners, he promised that if he could recruit 4,000 converts for his "Committee for Freedom Now" the civil rights battles could be won decisively. "You'll see a Negro councilman," he prophesied, "and if you want one, a Negro mayor!" During his haranguing

Stanley Branche and Dick Gregory. Photo by Jack T. Franklin, courtesy of the African American Museum in Philadelphia.

Chapter 8

criticism, Branche spared none of so-called elites of the race. The Rev. Donald Ming, pastor of Murphy AME Church and Chester Human Relations Committee head, filed libel charges against Branche, charging he publicly branded him an "Uncle Tom" and was burned in effigy at the instigation of Branche. The clergyman, who was scheduled to transfer to a Philadelphia pastorate, later made peace with Branche, becoming a brief ally.

"Stanley was needed here at this point," the clergyman declared shortly afterwards. "He exploited the white man's guilt. We needed to demonstrate; then afterwards, sit down and negotiate. We can't get all our demands at the same time."[3] That last sentence, by coincidence, was similar to one expressed in 1946 by the Rev. J. Pius Barbour, Calvary Baptist Church pastor, in an open letter addressed to young civil rights leaders at that time. (Herman Dawson, a businessman and a Calvary deacon, recalled Rev. Barbour's role* in the Sixties campaign. "He didn't march with us but we knew he was with us. We'd go to his home and talk for hours about strategy. He would tell us what to expect and how to react." It was later reported that "police had cracked Herman's skull" during a melee.)[4]

Through an obvious gesture of appeasement, Branche was given a seat on the Human Relations Committee after having accused the body of being unable to understand aspirations of local Blacks, and saying those Black members were not true representatives of the race. Disagreement and confusion on the committee resulted in almost wholesale resignations.

When Branche and his aide, Dr. Felder E. Rouse, Jr., a newcomer physician, quit the body only two members remained. Prior to leaving town, nonetheless, Rev. Ming initiated a thorough investigation of the de facto segregation practices of the school board.[5] The adamant school authorities had already announced

---

*Although Rev. Barbour never became a civil rights activist in the true sense of the term, the rest of his family made their contributions in the 1960s. His wife, Olee, and son, Pius, Jr., a physician, were active with the local NAACP; his daughter, Alminina, a lawyer, served on Martin Luther King, Jr.'s legal staff; the younger son, Littlejohn, was a Navy chaplain.

Politics and Prejudice

1964 PROTEST LEADERS AND SUPPORTERS: Mr. Garrison, Malcolm X, Gloria Richardson, unidentified man and Dick Gregory meet to discuss campaign to desegregate schools in Chester.
Photograph by Jack T. Franklin, courtesy of the African American Museum in Philadelphia.

they would not attempt to integrate faculties in predominantly white or Black neighborhoods. Such a move would prove too costly, the board reasoned.

Following a few heated negotiating sessions between Black leaders and school authorities, from which no rational agreement could be reached, battle lines were drawn for increased renewal of demonstrations. The ensuing events might be likened to forays which cast Branche and his motley regiments as representing a cross section of citizens, from south Chester to some of the surrounding boroughs. Their street opposition consisted of law enforcement minions and white citizen camp-followers opposed to race mixing. In the often violent confrontations, news correspondents and photographers were sometimes beaten and arrested for merely trying to carry out their duties. Communiques of the fast-paced civil rights battles spread across the nation through the media. Here, for example, are some brief summaries of reports in the *Delaware Country Daily Times*:

November 13, 1963—Franklin School was target of pickets protesting overcrowding and de facto segregation. Approx-

Chapter 8

imately 1,150 mostly Black students were enrolled at the school designed for a capacity of 980, necessitating classes being taught in the basement coal bin and at the nearby housing project. The demonstrators included white students from Swarthmore and Bryn Mawr colleges carrying signs reading "Black and White Together," "Now Is the Time" and "Down With Fake Arrests."

School Superintendent Charles Long promised that 170 pupils would be transferred and that the school would be closed "at some future date." In response, Dr. Nathaniel Plafker, Human Relations Committee chairman, called the proposed plan "forced integration and unwholesome." For this statement, the NAACP demanded his resignation. Plafker did resign later and joined forces with a white citizens group protesting integration.

November 18, 1963—Mayor Joseph Eyre said charges against 240 demonstrators already arrested would be dropped because the leaders promised picketing would cease.

April 1, 1964—Gloria Richardson, civil rights leader from Cambridge, Maryland, and the Rev. Clayton Hewet, of the Morton Episcopal Church, were among the 107 adults and 50 juveniles

Sit-down protest at 7th and Edgmont Streets, March 28, 1964. Photograph courtesy of Delaware County Historical Society, Pennsylvania.

Politics and Prejudice

Chester Committee for Freedom Now protesting circa April 26, 1964. Photograph by Jack T. Franklin, courtesy of the African American Museum in Philadelphia.

arrested when they emerged from a church rally and sat down in front of the police headquarters, protesting police treatment of marchers. The adults were bused to Broadmeadows Prison and the juveniles to Delaware County Children's College.

April 4, 1964—Civil rights leaders said they would halt demonstrations when they could meet with the school board. When this meeting was arranged, Rev. Ming and three Human Relations Committee members resigned because they were excluded from the session at the request of Branche and his group. Branche stated that the previous "agreement" about halting demonstrations was misunderstood. "We are not satisfied that the demonstrators have not been released as promised. There have been more than 200 confined at Broadmeadows over the past eight days."

April 6, 1964—Catherine Laws, retired school principal and funeral home owner elected last November to the school board, resigned. "I am not in favor of the steps you are taking," she told the members. "I am 100 percent for integration."

April 8, 1964—Clarence H. Roberts, long-time Black board member, declared no segregation existed in city schools. "If there

Chapter 8

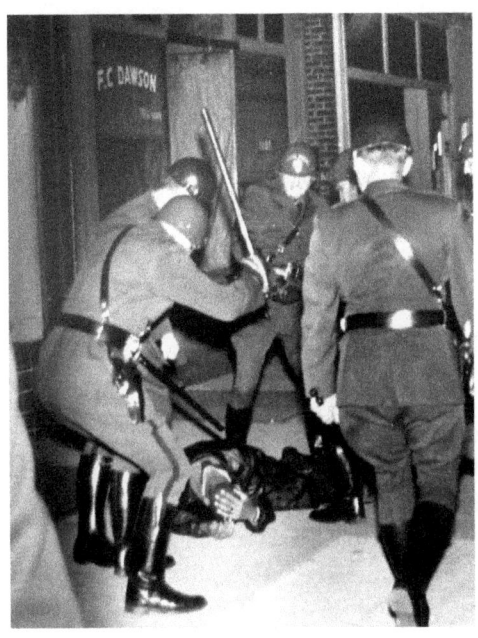

Police confront a Black man during disturbances of 1964. Photograph courtesy of Delaware County Historical Society, Pennsylvania.

are any shortcomings about an all-Black school, they can be traced to the principal. He is responsible. If he doesn't report it, our board is unaware of it. Our schools in all areas are integrated," he explained. At that time Watts, Franklin, Harvey, Douglass and Booker T. Washington schools had virtually all-Black enrollment.

April 22, 1964—All eighteen city schools were closed by order of the board, fearing more disorders and property damage. However, pickets demonstrated outside the school administration and municipal buildings.

April 23, 1964—City officials called in State Police. More than 215 demonstrators were arrested and 35 were injured, including Jack Franklin, a *Philadelphia Tribune* photographer. The homes of John J. McClure, the political boss, and school board member Clarence Roberts were picketed. James Farmer, head of the Congress of Racial Equality (CORE), spoke at a rally and John Lewis, chairman of the Student Nonviolent Coordinating Committee (SNCC), followed.

Ms. Eva Winters of Media offered her property deed to gain release of some of the jailed demonstrators, and Raymond announced the

121

NAACP had received $1,000 in contributions to help bail out the prisoners.

April 24, 1964—A threatened boycott by Blacks of over-town merchants was called off temporarily after a meeting between the Chester Businessmen's Association and the West End Ministerial Fellowship. The merchants were accused by Black leaders of hiring discrimination and of not using their influence in bringing about a solution to the racial controversy.

May 1, 1964—As ugly clashes between demonstrators and law enforcement showed no signs of abating (with State Police being called in at least four times since the previous November) the situation appeared to be getting out of hand. It was announced that the previous week, Protestant Episcopal Bishop Dr. Robert L. Dewitt and University of Pennsylvania Law School Dean Jefferson Fordham had driven from Philadelphia to Harrisburg at midnight, arousing Governor Scranton from bed to request his intervention into the Chester situation. Scranton, without hesitation, ordered the state Human Relations Commission to conduct a full-scale investigation into the matter.

May 4, 1964—At the initial meeting of the governor's Human Relations Commission, civil rights leaders (including Robert L. Carter, general counsel of the NAACP and three attorneys representing the local complainants) refused to participate claiming they had not received the legally required ten-day notice of the gathering. Nevertheless, Joseph X. Jaffee, Commission vice-chairman, voluntarily listed nine complaints against the school board in accordance with charges compiled earlier by its investigators. The principle complaints included maintenance of all-Black schools, assignment of Black teachers to all-Black schools, inferior education standards for Black schools, failure to appoint Blacks to administrative and supervisory positions, and gerrymandering of boundaries of school zones to perpetuate all-Black schools.

July 16, 1964—A meeting of the state Human Relations Commission, the school board and civil rights leaders broke up without reaching any sort of agreement. Philip Savage, NAACP representative, said he would make plans to have demonstrations resumed. Three school board members walked out, claiming the participants engaged in criticism of the board rather than considering a plan put forth by School Superintendent Long to end de facto segregation. After the Commission hearings ended, it ruled that the school board did in fact commit unlawful segregation as charged. Therefore the school authorities were ordered to eliminate all schools served by all-Black staffs and teachers and those housed in inferior buildings.

August 7, 1964—Acknowledging that the widespread demonstrations against school inadequacies and police brutality charges were symptoms of even more deep-rooted problems among Blacks, city business and commercial interests began efforts this week aimed at reforms. Governor Scranton arrived here, accompanied by five top aides, to help launch an ambitious experiment aimed at improving race relations and offering rejuvenation for long-neglected city services and facilities. The business-industrial leaders representing the power structure organized "The Greater Chester Movement," selecting a full-time executive secretary to man it. Nationally recognized industrialists Thomas B. McCabe, of Scott Paper, and J. Newton Pew, of the shipbuilding and oil conglomerate, would serve with the group whose chairman was Dr. Clarence R. Moll, Pennsylvania Military College president, who was active in bringing together warring factions in the school controversy.

In the absence of possibilities for any industrial development so badly needed, the movement leaders decided its secondary project would be considered. Two day-care centers for working mothers would be established. A clean-up, fix-up drive would be launched in rundown sections. The state Department of Public Instruction sent 1,000 books to help establish a new library in the deprived neighborhood. School facilities would be inventoried as a basis for renewal or rehabilitation. Federal agencies would be offering priorities for renewal projects, according to the planners. The undisciplined actions and appearances of policemen would be subject to reform, it was emphasized.[6]

For the beaten demonstrators either still in jail or under indictment, such a pledge offered very little consolation.

Leo S. Holmes.

Schools Ordered Integrated

Exactly one year after the demonstrations at Franklin School the state Human Relations Commission, noting that the school board "continues to commit unlawful acts of discrimination that deprive Negroes of their civil rights,"[7] ordered the authorities to submit by January 31, 1965 plans for the desegregation of the five elementary schools and one junior high school in question. The board, interestingly, selected as its president Clarence Roberts, its veteran member who once denied discrimination existed in local schools.[8]

His appetite apparently whetted for more civil rights battles, Branche moved to Philadelphia where he joined the campaign against Girard College which had barred Blacks under a legal stipulation left in the will of its founder.[9] However, back in Chester, his prediction to his followers that they would have a Black city councilman did come to pass in the election (political selection, to be sure) of Leo Holmes, a math instructor.[10] Moreover, it appeared highly possible that in face of the new militancy evidenced among Blacks, the political bosses were at last beginning to heed their demands for more representation in decision-making positions. So, it was around this period that Robert A. Wright, the first Black to pass the county bar examination, was appointed an assistant county district attorney.¹¹

The adamant school board, having persuaded two lower courts that the state Human Relations Commission had no authority to order any desegregation ruling, finally lost its challenge when in September, 1967, the state supreme court overruled the two lower courts. In reply, the school board voted to prepare its plan to "eliminate or reduce substantially racial imbalance" in the six schools cited in the case.¹²

The curious legal threats hanging over the heads of 300 citizen-demonstrators who helped forge this victory did not disappear until early 1971 when the District Attorney's office decided to drop all charges brought seven years earlier. All had been free on bond or on their recognizance.¹³

When the Greater Chester venture was launched, many of its local sponsors were in a large sense responsible for the serious plight involving high unemployment and related problems (problems which added to the low morale they would address). Beginning in the mid-1960s, more than 5,000 jobs were lost when big industries such as Ford Motors, Atlantic Steel and Reynolds Metals abandoned town, and Sun Ship, Scott Paper and Boeing Aircraft cut back their work forces. Moreover, 250 small- and medium-sized retail businesses, often facing threats of boycotts or picketing by jobless Blacks, also closed their doors in face of declining sales. Market Street and Edgmont Avenue, long the sites of successful department stores, movie theaters, restaurants and 5-and-10 stores, were now homes to a few cut-rate stores, thrift shops or haberdasheries catering mainly to young, sporty customers. Several of the businesses were owned or operated by Asian families. Few Blacks worked in these new types of small enterprises.

The city's overall jobless rate was 8%, yet estimated to be double that among Blacks (whose families represented 26% of those living below the federal poverty level). The population of Blacks, for reasons not patently clear, had doubled in the postwar decade to 42%. One scholar made an attempt to answer the question by making a study of factors contributing to migration patterns among whites and nonwhites (98% Blacks). His findings:

Politics and Prejudice

OLD MARKET STREET, once the city's principal business district, now the location of "cut-rate" and bargain basement shops. Renamed "Avenue of the States."

— 14.5% non-whites came to seek employment, compared to 8% whites.

— 10% non-whites came to live with families, compared to 17% whites.

— 53% non-whites came for reasons of family ties and jobs, compared to 35% whites.

— 9% non-whites had definite job offers, compared to 15% whites.

"Chester had emerged from the Second World War with high potential and hope," the researcher stated, offering his rationale. "The community was in an abundance of natural resources, a reservoir of skilled manpower, adequate rail facilities, a strong educational system, branches of nationwide industries and an ever-widening market area. City leaders spoke in glowing terms of the economic future.... Unfortunately, the promise was never fulfilled. Instead, the city's physical facilities and human capital were gradually dissipated by 'dynamic forces' in our economic system.

"Some measure of blame," the report continued, "may lie with local political and industrial leaders who did not anticipate these forces or develop accommodative plans. Representatives of the poor blamed the powers-that-be for the city's decline, while those factions charged that widespread poverty and joblessness was the fault of those affected who failed to take advantages because of personal laziness or sloth or to an excessively liberal public

Chapter 8

welfare policy."[14]

In his particular reference to a "strong education system," the author of the study, John T. Meli, a product of a longtime politically connected family, tended to illustrate the myoptic, racially biased view of his ilk. To virtually every knowledgeable citizen it was a known fact that Blacks were never afforded adequate academic or vocational training in city schools, thus rendering them unqualified for scores of decent jobs. Indeed, at the period of Mr. Meli's study, school authorities were vigorously opposing education reforms ordered by the courts.

NEW BLACK LEADERSHIP CADRE EMERGES
Bibliography

1. *Delaware County Daily Times,* March 25, 1965.

2. *New York Times,* May 1, 1964.

3. Ibid, February 13, 1964.

4. Kirk B. Jones, "Black Pastors/Public Life," *Christian Century Magazine,*

September 13, 1989, p. 17.

5. *New York Times,* May 5, 1965.

6. Ibid, August 7, 1964.

7. Ibid, November 20, 1964.

8. Ibid, December 7, 1966.

9. Ibid, May 4, 1966.

10. Ibid, November 4, 1965.

11. *Delaware County Times,* August 6, 1970.

12. *New York Times,* September 26, 1967.

13. Ibid, February 14, 1971.

14. John T. Meli, "Barriers To Employment—Growth in a Depressed Area," 1972, Unpublished MS thesis, Widener College.

Chapter 9

The Controversial John Nacrelli Decade (1971-80)

MAYOR CONVICTED FOR BRIBERY; BLACKS GAIN FEW POLITICAL PLUMS

Given the ebb and flow of events, the seventies in all probability spelled the city's most crucial decade thus far. This was especially true regarding Blacks, increasingly becoming the majority. Yet they were still lacking strong, unfettered leadership in the policy-making quarters—the legal ones, that is. True, a few of the political-minded did gain a bit of recognition, albeit through the grace of the machine, although some occasionally reacted in a manner not unlike certain human beings faced with irresistible temptations.

The masses, on the other hand, faced serious shortages in employment and housing. An overabundance of crime and vice continued to spread while the law enforcement unit had to concentrate on keeping its house in order, busily protecting its reputation against the peculiar vagaries of the city's chief executive. Fortunately for the citizenry, federal and state authorities began making their presence felt in such matters. Joblessness generally breeds crime, yet some of the nefarious activities of a handful of cops had the tendency to hasten breakdowns in respect for the law by individuals already especially amenable to committing criminal misdeeds.

Vastly improved education facilities and curricula did not necessarily signal increases in vocational or professional opportunities, for as the first blush of a new high school began wearing thin, some students, upon observing the scarcity in the local job market, retired to street idleness and its subsequent allure. Civic-minded parental guidance, nonetheless, might prevent such youthful leakage.

On the positive side of the ledger, a fresh sense of racial cooperation appeared strongly evident. Now that segregation in housing and schools were legally outlawed, white and Black families had chances of getting to know each other better. No longer could the age-old tactic of "divide and conquer" by vested interests be wholly successful. White clergy folk extended financial as well as spiritual support for new housing for Blacks, and some encouraged others to take up residences in hitherto exclusively "white" county towns.

The Wright Clan Rises

The saga of the Wright clan is one that eventually forced the GOP king-makers to consider public sentiment among Blacks and offer a certain degree of appeasement in the form of higher types of patronage for their qualified, faithful leaders. Unlike many other politically-connected citizens, the father, son and grandson served prominently in the local NAACP and other civic organizations. E. Courtlandt Wright, the low-key pillar of the community with a political following, was ultimately named executive director of the important city Redevelopment Authority after having been given several meaningless appointments over the past years.

His son, Robert A., a Lincoln University graduate, was the first of his race to pass the county bar after finishing the Temple University Law School. He served as legal advisor to the NAACP during the 1964 integration battles and was one of the two Black attorneys the county "War Board" planned to name as a county assistant district attorney. The move was seen by some as a ploy aimed at trying to mollify the increasingly volatile Black citizens. Reliable reports filtered out that board members were trying to decide whether to tap Wright or Palmer Hunt, the other candidate, also a Black. John J. McClure, ailing and aged, came down on the side of "Bob" Wright, explaining that Lewis M. Hunt, uncle of Palmer, had received many favors from the machine in the past, but that "Court" Wright had been favored so few times.

Even prior to Boss McClure's demise in 1965, there had been calls for a Black to serve as a county Common Pleas Court judge. Invariably, one would first have to be appointed to an unexpired term before facing county-wide voters as a Black for a first full term with GOP blessings. When the War Board tapped James H. Gorbey, former Chester mayor, to move from his Common Pleas seat to a federal judgeship, a possible opening appeared for Wright to receive his prize.

Plans for both maneuvers hit a temporary snag when Dr. Felder Rouse and Stanley C. Branche, leaders of the school strike, appeared at a Philadelphia hearing concerning Gorbey's qualifications, protesting his elevation, citing some of his "heavy-handed" action during the school demonstrations, and holding him responsible for hundreds of arrests and police brutality allegations. The general understanding was that should Gorbey fail to get his appointment, there would be no Common Pleas Court bench for Wright. Injecting himself and his organization into the controversy, George Raymond, NAACP president and long-time friend of Wright, wrote authorities, protesting that neither Rouse nor Branche represented his organization as they reportedly claimed at the hearing. Paradoxically, this represented a left-handed endorsement for Gorbey from Raymond, even though he had always been in general agreement with both Rouse and Branche on civic matters. More important, the matter had been a critical boost for Wright who had been passed over several times when openings on the bench occurred. By now, in addition to increased endorsements from groups other than Blacks, including the Polish National Alliance, the controversy spread county-wide.[1]

As the debate dragged on over the months, the War Board found itself facing two crucial facts: Democratic Governor Milton Schapp, who would assume office January 1, 1971, could pass the federal judgeship to a Democrat; and many important county GOP stalwarts expressed concern that if Wright was not appointed, Blacks could bolt the party. Without wasting any more time, the power brokers settled on His Honor Common Pleas Court Judge Robert A. Wright.[2]

Judge Wright's son, Robert C., a graduate of Villanova Law School, was admitted to the county bar in 1970, and served numerous community agencies, as well as teaching school in Chester Township before winning a special election as state representative for District 159.

As Bob Wright began his tenure on the Common Pleas Court, a man many Blacks considered their best friend in Media, Judge Henry G. Sweney, was retiring after serving twenty-nine years.

Chapter 9

John "Jack" Nacrelli, Chester mayor and political boss.

Sweney would unceremoniously throw out cases prosecutors brought before him if he considered any were unfair—instances which happened more than once involving Black defendants. He once resigned from the YMCA Board because it did not take fast enough action in constructing the West End Branch Y, for which Blacks had raised their share of building funds. Although originally appointed to the bench by the McClure faction, he was a man of independent thought and action throughout his tenure. Here is how he was lauded by an admirer at his retirement banquet:

"He came to the court in a period of changing values, changing philosophies, political and economic unrest, and these imponderables were augmented and multiplied over the years in this and other courts over the nation ... no man stood taller in meeting these challenges than did Judge Sweney."[3]

Mayoral, Police Scandals

Just as the long public careers of the Wrights were exemplar of service to the public, the controversial decade of John H. Nacrelli, a man of the same political sponsorship, was clouded with crime and corruption that led to his eventual imprisonment. A protege of McClure and his immediate successors, Nacrelli enjoyed a meteoric rise through the ranks by way of a variety of jobs that included manager of the then jim-crow McCaffery Housing Project, county assessor aide, city Recreation Director, and a Chester Housing Authority member.[4] Later he received appointment as a city councilman. In less than two years, he moved into the mayor's seat when John Gorbey resigned to accept his Common Pleas Court judgeship in 1968.

Nacrelli meanwhile busied himself overseeing the federal assurance of a $6.5 million redevelopment program for the central city, the work to cover the subsequent five years. The few undertakings in south Chester tended to be negated by the long-time construction work on U.S. Route 95 and the Commodore Barry Bridge, causing the uprooting of scores of businesses. Several neighborhood mini-parks were constructed, the most notable probably being the Ethel Waters Park, dedicated to the Chester-born singer-actress.

In the matter of law enforcement, the police department cited the mayor as the "man of the year" for instigating a training program and expanding its 92-man personnel to 127 in 1970. In less than a decade, nonetheless, police staffing was reduced to its original 90-plus, the announced reason being budgetary rather than morale. Yet despite the population drop from 56,633 in 1970 to 45,859 in that period, the city saw a substantial increase in major crimes, such as murder, manslaughter, aggravated assault, rape, burglary, robbery, theft and larceny. At the same time, the police bureau that clearly became the mayor's pride and joy, often became saddled with its own recurring scandals, both internally and externally. It was a seeming paradox that the law enforcement units and some of its political cohorts would—directly or not—eventually be involved in Nacrelli's downfall. Some Blacks indeed were partners

Partnership headquarters of Leroy Miah, the former policeman who had a bitter feud with city officials for several years.

in crime with the mayor while others came off as victims.

There was, for instance, the strange, intriguing case of Patrolman Leroy Miah, who along with two Chester Township policemen, was convicted of driving a vehicle through a state-owned liquor store in 1971, then burglarizing it. Some persons in the know felt that Miah's police career had actually started downhill after leading a raid against a gambling joint believed to be run by Frank Miller, the gambling boss. During Miah's three, long drawn-out trials, several other policemen testified against him. One swore he witnessed eight other policemen dividing the stolen liquor among themselves in Miah's private garage; nevertheless none of them were charged, and one refused to testify in any of Miah's trials. By 1973 Miah was put in solitary confinement at the county prison, and ultimately prepared a post-conviction petition, but claimed he could not find a lawyer willing to handle the matter. "They wouldn't let this get into court because there were too many people involved," he stated later.[5] (Years later, Miah organized the "Miah and Sanbe Hauling Contractors" business, handling numerous contracts with the city.)

At one time Detective Sergeant Commodore Harris, Jr. publicly alleged that he and another Black policeman were taken to Mayor Nacrelli by Herman Fontaine, a GOP committeeman and Frank Miller partner. They were offered a political "promotion" to go easy on the "Miller-Fontaine" policy business, but crack down on any rivals. Harris said he refused.[6] There had been further assertions that some policemen were serving as Fontaine's bodyguards.

Also during Nacrelli tenure, Robert Kinlaw, a thirty-year veteran who reached the post of inspector, was indicted by a federal grand jury for allegedly operating a policy syndicate. Kinlaw, father of four college-educated girls and a GOP committeeman, was also the senior among the three inspectors eligible to become the next chief of police. Lieutenant Bill Riley, president of the Delaware County Black Policemen's Association, which strongly campaigned for equality in the police adminstration, condemned the indictment. He averred some of "our members even jeopardize their own chances of moving up the politically-braced ladder by calling for the resignation of Mayor Nacrelli," citing corruption at City Hall.[7]

Son-in-law of veteran policeman Leroy Richardson, Riley, who would attempt to run for mayor in the future,[8] pointed out that mere charges or indictments, particularly against public servants, generally leave a negative implication even if the person is proven innocent. "The whole system is often held in disrespect when several law enforcement members have their badges tarnished under such circumstances," opined Riley.

Another suspicious incident became public in 1977 when Patrolman William Parker, another Black, was discharged for "blowing the whistle" on an attempted cover-up involving Mayor Nacrelli's daughter. Parker, distraught with failure to find another job, committed suicide. Later, a federal jury found that the mayor and others in the police department did conspire to dismiss Parker because he cooperated with the FBI investigation of a suspected drug case. Parker's widow, Gertrude, was awarded $50,000 in damages, including $25,000 in compensary damages from the city, plus additional punitive damages of $5,000 apiece from Nacrelli, city Councilman Leo S. Holmes, ex-councilman Jimmie Sharpe (both Blacks), and patrolman Alexander Osowski.[9] Whether or not due to the ongoing federal probe, a mild shakeup was undertaken by Police Chief William Hoopes, the last white to head the department for a while. One of his moves was to appoint as acting captain Floyd Lewis, one of the first local Blacks to serve with the State Police.[10]

After a long, intensive investigation, a federal grand jury convicted Mayor Nacrelli in February, 1979, on tax evasion, bribery and racketeering. Primarily he was convicted of accepting $22,000 in protection money from gambling figures Frank Miller and Herman Fontaine. The U.S. Attorney's office said numerous payments were given the mayor by Miller and Fontaine for protecting their illicit syndicate.[11] Miller and his partner were previously convicted for their roles. Nacelle was sentenced to six years in Allenwood Federal Prison, plus five years probation. He was released in 1982, with the stipulation he be barred from holding public office until 1992.

Again, a year after Nacrelli's conviction, twenty-six policemen were furloughed—for economic reasons, it was reported.

In conjunction with the conviction of Miller, a resident of Chester Township, the government could not confiscate any of his property obtained with friends or relatives as "fronts" or cooperators. These holdings included seventy-three pieces of real estate, four bars and an oil company, most having been purchased with "hard cash."[12] By coincidence or not, Otto Fontaine, a one-time policeman and a nephew of Herman, was married to Miller's daughter.

Herman Fontaine, a hail-well-met fellow whose official role was that of a GOP committeeman and sometimes bar operator, nonetheless could always be depended upon to make donations to youth programs or civic causes. In fact, he earned the nickname "Coach" while playing and helping Henry "Alex" Hunt coach the Central Boys Club football team in the early 1940s. A member of an early, well-respected Chester family, his eldest brother, Dr. William Fontaine, culminated a distinguished career as a philosophy professor at the University of Pennsylvania.

School System Finally Overhauled

In the aftermath of decades of bitter demonstrations, city public school facilities were finally integrated from kindergarten through high school, as were the faculty and administration. Furthermore, with the exception of Booker T. Washington, constructed in 1923, all the old plants were closed permanently or demolished. The venerable old Chester High, standing since 1901, was mysteriously destroyed by fire in 1968, one year after the state supreme court ordered the stubborn school board to desegregate, the latter having exhausted all appeals.

A completely revamped system consisted of six elementary schools, three middle schools (grades 7-9), and a new $22 million state-of-the art high school. Of the two former junior high schools, Smedley was named as one of the three newly designated middle schools, the others being Pulaski and Showalter. Douglass, built in 1932, was abandoned and sold as a private community-based facility. The original five-member school board merged in 1972 with the adjoining borough, then becoming the nine-member Chester-Upland Board. Clarence Roberts continued as board president.

Politics and Prejudice

Jessie B. Powell

The first graduating class of the new high school in 1974 was dominated by 480 Blacks. The first Black principal was Eugene Johnson, succeeded by Ms. Jessie Powell, both products of local schools.[13] Four years later when the facility shakedown was complete Chester High had 200 instructors and 3,200 students. Harold Smith, another local Black, eventually became school superintendent, succeeding John Vaul who, as Dewey-Mann Elementary School principal in 1946, opposed enrolling Blacks in his facility.[14]

By the time of the 1978-79 school year, Black students accounted for 79% of the city's public school enrollment.[15] Later, the high school enrollment would decline despite continued increase in the overall Black population. Interestingly, some Black parents, for various reasons—none altogether religious—were sending their children to Catholic schools. No accurate count, however, could be obtained concerning the number of Blacks enrolled.

For what it is worth, there were two past singular cases that might illustrate some ramifications of segregated schools versus parental influence. During the school controversy of the mid-1940s two leaders, it may be recalled, were Mesdames Frinjella Bond and Ethel Brown. Mrs. Bond and her husband, Cecil, Sr., kept their five sons in public school while fighting for equal education. Mr. and Mrs. William Brown later enrolled their son and daughter in a local school. The Bond boys continued through Chester High following in the footsteps of their father, a former basketball star there. The Brown daughter, Ethel, later attended an Ivy League college and became a lawyer, and her granddaughter a doctor in Maryland.[16] William Brown, Jr. and his son, William III, were elected to city governmental positions; the father as a regional court justice, and son "Rocky," who was also a minister, as city controller. The adult Bonds, Cecil, Jr., Carl, Ronald, Rodney and Clyde,[17] found professional positions in such important businesses as the Southeastern Pennsylvania Transit Authority, Philadelphia Municipal Stadium, Coca-Cola Company, the State Police and Sears Roebuck, all located in Philadelphia.

New Housing Constructed

One might well wonder why the shortage of affordable housing for Blacks existed in a city whose total population nose-dived from approximately 66,000 to 43,000 within twenty years. The logical explanation was that Blacks, arriving as fast as whites were leaving the city, were moving into many of the houses abandoned by the latter group in various sections of the town. Yet, as more than 53 percent of all homes had been built in 1939 or earlier,[18] many were long neglected and almost beyond repair. Others in fair condition called for rents out of the reach of many of the unemployed and those families living below the federal poverty level. Furthermore, out of the 17,000 residences, 1,400 were condemned or substandard.[19]

As jobless rates for Blacks were nearly doubling those of whites, the crying need for low-rent housing had become desperate, including cases of the elderly and handicapped citizens. A long history of housing discrimination finally came to an end when the city was forced to permit Blacks to occupy two public housing projects, McCaffery Village and William Penn, the latter located in a neighborhood from which Blacks had been relocated. Thanks largely to available federal funds, the Chester Housing Authority sponsored, in 1971, the 296-unit high-rise "Twin Towers" complex for the elderly located on Edgmont Avenue across from the historic Deshong Art Gallery and Park. The living quarters were divided into 121 studio apartments and 175 with one bedroom.

Thus, along with other low-rent projects, the Housing Authority theoretically offered 2,668 homes, although scores of units in the original projects were constantly too damaged for occupation, many by vandalization.[20]

The West End Ministerial Fellowship, composed of twenty-seven clergymen, purchased three acres of land from the city in 1970, planning for the first construction of private homes in the Ninth Ward since 1960. Seed money was contributed primarily by white religious groups—Quakers, Methodists, Presbyterians and Baptists—from both Upland and Swarthmore, one church lending $20,000 interest-free. Fifty-four homes with three and four bedrooms in the $19-22,000 price range were ultimately constructed on West Ninth Street between Tilghman and Yarnall. The dominating force behind the undertaking was the Rev. Daniel A. Scott, Bethany Baptist Church pastor and the Fellowship president.

This was the period when the U.S. 95 highway running from Philadelphia through Chester and the Commodore Barry Bridge were under construction, resulting in the uprooting of some 132 families. "These families who were notified to move didn't have anywhere to go," Rev. Scott explained at the time. "If they had to leave town they would have started a pattern and our churches would be emptied."[21] The new Martin Luther King Homes were ready for occupancy in 1973. A few years later, a new 72-unit housing development was named the Daniel A. Scott Commons[22] in honor of the clergyman. Scott was a member of the city Human Relations Committee and one of the founders of the local OIC (Opportunities Industrialization Center) whose original headquarters were in Scott's church quarters.

An "up-to-date environment for handicapped folks to live with self-reliance and dignity" was the primary reason for construction of the Stinson Towers in 1978 at Arbor Drive and West Fifteenth Street. The 13-story, 150-unit high-rise consisted of 90 efficiency, 57 one-bedroom and two-bedroom apartments that offered a wide variety of conveniences and services for its handicapped and blind tenants, whose ages ranged from twenty-two to eighty-five years. The towers featured special raised dials on telephones,

Chapter 9

A few of the relatively new residential homes for Blacks in the Ninth Ward.

handrails along corridors and ramps in and out of the building, plus a twenty-four-hour security system and a medical office serviced twice weekly by a visiting doctor and nurse.

Rentals for the units, subsidized by the U.S. Department of Housing and Urban Development, ranged from $360 to $472 monthly, but tenants were required to pay 25 percent of their annual income, with HUD supplying the remainder. In addition to the Robert H. Stinson Association, prime mover, the project was completed with the cooperation of the county branch of the Pennsylvania

Benjamin Bannecker Plaza.

139

Raleigh Merrick, developer, enjoys a moment with the owner of one of the homes his company built.

Association for the Blind, the Chester Lions Club and the State Housing Finance Agency.[23]

Also moving into the breach to help alleviate housing shortages was the Quaker-sponsored Robert Wade Neighborhood House, an organization with a long history of community services to the race. After several years of sometimes spurious opposition by a few Blacks, plans were finally approved by the Federal Housing Authority to construct the proposed Benjamin Banneker Plaza at Seventh Street at Engle, with one of its consultants being Wilson Goode, future mayor of Philadelphia.[24] The area for the planned building had long been devoid of residential housing, yet during one of the series of public hearings, one man said he was against low-cost public housing because "people throw whiskey bottles on your property." A more articulate woman stated, "We are opposed to a six-story apartment building. It would be detrimental to the community. We are asking for the type of housing that will conform with the existing homes in the neighborhood, which are two-story, not six."[25]

These arguments indeed seemed strangely reminiscent of those launched in the distant past, yet which ceased when the dominant political machine was assured patronage control of federally funded housing. It had already been publicized that the homes were not designed to become low-cost public housing; rather, they were intended to fall into the gap between public and middle-income units. Following numerous setbacks, the seventy-apartment complex consisting of two buildings was finally dedicated in May, 1977, nearly six years after it was first proposed. Its board of directors included Dr. Felder Rouse and Mrs. Ella Bryant, both civic activists.

Original rent scale was to be from $131.50 to $160 monthly for the one- and two-bedroom apartments; but rents soon began skyrocketing, and conflicts arose between tenants and management over various complaints. Whether or not these differences were resolved, the Banneker Plaza was acquired by the National Corporation of Housing Partnership of Washington, D. C., in 1980.[28] The project continued to offer decent housing for those families for which it was intended. Possibly as an added bonus for tenants was the proximity of a spacious city park and the J. Lewis Crozer Library, a favorite institution in the community for nearly fifty years.

Some Blacks who managed to improve their economic outlook more than the average during wartime also sought new environs that were fortunately found in the up-and-coming Excelsior Village[27] a 45-home development in Upper Chichester, just west of Chester's border. This was the longtime dream of Raleigh Merrick, a Philadelphia realtor who purchased several acres of farmland and began building homes in 1941, matching the tastes and bank accounts of middle-class Blacks. A stranger passing through the tract of handsome homes—many with unique alabaster statues, bird baths and neatly manicured lawns—might have wrongly assumed it to be a white neighborhood.

Merrick's wife, Agnes, a music teacher, explained their plans and motivation for the tightly-knit community. "After the first residents moved in, we formed a committee to check on the maintenance of the grounds. The folks were strict about keeping up the area," she added, "because they had a hard time finding a nice place and wanted to keep it that way. We organized a civic association which involved the entire community, even the children." The couple, married more than fifty years and parents of two sons, said they hoped the children living in the village would be motivated by the thrift and other examples of citizenship illustrated by the adult citizens.

The last homes were constructed in 1972, yet one of the first ones built in the 1940s for $4,000 sold for $40,000 in 1974. Merrick's advice was sought in the planning and development of the Martin Luther King Homes. "Some of the homeowners in that project came to see Excelsior Village and wanted to do the same things there," he said. "They already have formed a civic association."[28]

THE CONTROVERSIAL JOHN NACRELLI DECADE
Bibliography

1. *Delaware County Daily Times*, November 30, 1970.

2. Ibid, December 28, 1970.

3. Ibid, January 17, 1971.

4. Ibid, November 5, 1967.

5. Ibid, May 3, 1978. Miah's version as told to a *Times* columnist.

6. Ibid, November 5, 1967.

7. Ibid, "City Lines" column by John Roman, March 10, 1978.

8. Ibid, July 20, 1983.

9. Ibid, November 2, 1983.

10. Ibid, August 25, 1978.

11. Ibid, February 7, 1979.

12. Ibid, May 3, 1978.

13. Chester-Upland School District Report.

14. R. E. Harris, *Delinquency In Our Democracy* (Philadelphia: Wetzel Publishing, 1954), p. 21.

15. Chester-Upland School District Report, 1980.

16. Interview with Mrs. Brown by author.

17. Interview with Mrs. Bond-Watson by author.

18. U.S. Census on Housing.

Chapter 9

19. Chester Housing Authority Report, 1980.

20. Ibid.

21. *Delaware County Daily Times*, December 16, 1973.

22. *Delaware County Daily Times*, November 20, 1983.

23. Ibid, July 27, 1978.

24. Ibid, August 5, 1971.

25. Ibid, May 2, 1977.

26. Ibid, January 14, 1980.

27. Ibid, April 30, 1974.

28. Interviews with the Merricks by author, May, 1989.

Chapter 10

First Black Woman Appointed Mayor (1981-90)

McCLURE HEIRS STILL INSIST ON DOMINATING CITY

As usual, the appointment procedure, so much a part of the political machine's modus operandi, resulted in the tapping of Joseph Battle in 1980 as the mayor to succeed the convicted John Nacrelli. But Battle, possibly more professionally qualified as a city chief executive than many of his predecessors, faced the difficult task of having to preside over a municipality "sinking so deeply in economic problems that it couldn't go anywhere but up," as one minor official put it.[1]

However, the shrewd tricks Battle learned as a young lawyer out of the University of Pennsylvania while sitting in on McClure's "War Board" would be of little benefit to him now that he was on his own in a more complex era. He admired the "old man," as he referred to John McClure,[2] who despite brushes with the law had been recipient of an honorary doctorate from the Pennsylvania Military College and the Kiwanis Merit Award for Public Service in 1961.

Shortly after winning his first two-year term, Battle began a struggle to restore the city's credibility and reputation to the days prior to the corruption scandals. To his apparent surprise, the city GOP executive committee's ninety-four members elected Doris Nacrelli, ex-mayor John's wife, vice chairman.[3] Curiously enough, Battle, the nominal chairman, said he was unaware of the contemplated move, which could undermine his authority, as at least three of the city council members were controlled by the Nacrelli faction.[4]

The already severe unemployment situation was in desperate straits when Sun Shipyard, the area's largest employer, announced a layoff of 3,000 workers in early 1981.[5] "This is going to have a catastrophic effect...," Battle complained. "Even prior to this, we were one of the most depressed cities in the nation." He noted that 16,000 of the 45,000 adult residents were already on welfare rolls. Furthermore, Blacks represented approximately 65 percent of the population and 32 percent of them were considered living below the federal poverty level.[6]

The city sought assistance from the county, state and federal governments in various ways. Governor Richard Thornburg directed his economic development committee to establish job-placement and counseling services to cooperate with local authorities in efforts to promote recovery. The state Department of Labor tabbed the official jobless rate at 10 percent. The mayor said it was 14 percent and other estimates place that of Black teenagers as high as 40 percent. "The state stops counting when people give up and stop looking for jobs," the city economic development director opined.[7]

As an example of just how threadbare Chester's businesses were, one might cite a comparison with York, Pennsylvania, a slightly smaller city:[8]

	Chester	York
Population	45,045	44,300
Retail employees	1,304	2,929
Merchandizing stores	40	176
Apparel	88	343

Though not nearly as much as in industry, the decline in retail businesses obviously affected residents to a significant degree. First, plummeting sales reduced taxes to the city treasury, thus reducing services and personnel, including the 25 percent of the police force that Battle temporarily furloughed.[9] The situation moreover posed problems for many shoppers, whether they dealt in cash or food stamps at small but more costly "mom-and-pop" neighborhood stores. Because no shopping malls existed in Chester, many residents were forced to travel to Brookhaven, Upland or Claymont, Delaware, to find bargains. Senior citizens, fortunately, had one money-saving advantage—SEPTA bus rides for them were free between 9:00 A.M. and 3:00 P.M.

Shopping conditions represented a far cry from the days when spans of Third Street, Central Avenue and a portion of West

Lower sections of West Third Street, former area of white ethnics, now dominated by Blacks.

Ninth Street flourished with a fairly large number of convenient shopping outlets, including the popular "American" and "Atlantic and Pacific" stores, butcher shops, fish markets, pharmacies, hardwares, fruit stands and restaurants. Third Street, in particular, between Tilghman and Yarnell, was something of a smaller Lennox

Avenue. Shopping indeed was a "movable feast" for all.

Some former habitués blamed the start of construction on the Commodore Barry Bridge for the eventual demise of this liveliest of the Black sectors. Many months of work on the bridge that ultimately crossed the Delaware River to New Jersey necessitated the blocking-off of Third Street for long periods of time, and also eliminated the homes of professionals residing on the south side of Flower Street, where the bridge passed overhead.

The city which had been subjected to paradoxical events over the past several decades, witnessed the shifting of remaining Black businesses farther south on West Third Street, occupying buildings abandoned by the ethnic residents—Polish, Ukrainians, Italians, etc. One building with the name POLISH-AMERICAN CITIZENS CLUB emblazoned high across its front became a social club for Blacks who previously avoided that unfriendly area for years. The John A. Watts Elks Lodge and the Franklin F. and A. M. Masonic Lodge headquarters were among the older, popular fraternal organizations that relocated in the stretch situated roughly between Yarnell Street and Highland Avenue.

Crime Wave Spreads

Lawlessness, generally a natural by-product of unemployment, tormented the city in most of the eighties, yet hopeful signs appeared near the decade's end that some categories might begin to decrease:[10]

Year	Pop.	Cops	Homicide	Rape	Assault	Robbery	Burglary	Motor Theft	Arson
1981	45,859	90	19	69	915	485	1,916	383	113
1983	45,744	102	15	63	952	403	1,447	336	
1984	45,045	101	13	112	1,026	372	1,317	405	26
1986	44,029	104	12	74	1,384	354	1,309	543	
1988	44,396	89	9	66	1,487	311	915	676	20
2006*	36,695		18	21	704	241	444	284	25

*2006 data, the most recent available, were added to this edition for purposes of comparison.

The number of criminal arrests, as submitted by the city to the U.S. Uniform Crime Report annually, does not show those directly related to illegal drug trafficking, though much of the overall criminal activity is presumed to be the cause or effect of the prevalent drug culture. For example, certain drugs such as marijuana or angel dust have been known to incite homicide, aggravated assaults, sexual crimes, etc. Many drug users turn to robbery, burglary, car thefts and other property crimes in order to support their habits. Moreover, some stimulant drugs are said to be highly correlated to teen-age and adolescent pregnancy, poor grades and school dropouts.

Like in many urban areas across the nation, low-rent housing projects in Chester had the tendency to serve as fertile fields for drug pushers as well as users. Captain Commodore Harris, Jr., head of the local police Narcotic Division, once named the William Penn and the Ruth L. Bennett housing projects as the most notorious in this category.[11] As trafficking increased, young pushers could be spotted along streets in north and south Chester peddling their wares, even in broad daylight. Some users waylaid pedestrians to get their needed cash, and some pushers did not have to resort to violence for their dubious success. Business types, Black or white, male or female, were their customers who knew on what corner or nook pushers hung out while looking for sales.

Police were ever on the lookout for drug offenders and yet it might sometimes have been rather difficult for a not-too-young policeman to chase and capture some of the young "speed merchants." City inspectors could—and did—obtain orders to demolish vacant buildings often used as "shooting galleries." If Captain Harris and his squad were not certain of obtaining the proper evidence to shut down a commercial hangout of suspected narcotics offenders, they were often able to see that the place was padlocked on safety or sanitary violations, as decided by appropriate city inspectors.[12] The city also instituted a curfew for those under eighteen years of age requiring them to be off the streets by 9:30 P.M. Sunday through Thursday and 11:30 P.M. Friday and Saturday.

As it did so prevalently from the Depression thirties onward, the policy or numbers game and other illicit rackets again tended to capitalize on the poor, particularly Blacks hoping to strike it rich or at least win enough cash to tide their families over for another week or two. The Battle administration faced evidence of a gambling conspiracy revival that ultimately led to the downfall of the previous mayor. This time rumors began spreading that Philadelphia mobs controlled the action. The finger-pointing brought back reminders of the fifties when the Philadelphia district attorney charged, in part, "it was common knowledge that if you wanted to engage in the numbers or horse-racing business in Chester you had to see ... political bosses." In October, 1983,[13] more than fifty lawmen staged gambling raids at homes and establishments on West Second, Third and Fourth Streets in the south Chester section, proving that gambling was still an ongoing vocation. The State Crime Commission launched its own investigation, the findings to be made public many months later.

On the matter of troublesome migrations from the City of Brotherly Love, several families of the notorious "MOVE" back-to-nature cult resided in Chester at the time (May, 1985) when scores of Philadelphia homes were incinerated in attempts to eradicate the group from its fortress-like abode. On suspicion that a house on McIlvain Street served as a refuge for cult members escaping the Philadelphia conflagration, Battle ordered police to evict the family of Alphonso Robbins, alias Moe Africa. Moe could not be located, but police took his wife, Mary Africa, and five children in custody, turning over the offspring to the county Children and Youth Services. Their former home was later demolished. Neighbors condemned authorities for the entire episode with such denunciations as, "They haven't bothered nobody," "I didn't hear nobody go in there and say 'What you are doing is illegal,'" "They endangered those people's lives," and "It was stupid. Mayor Battle just wanted to get in on the action between MOVE and the Philly police."[14]

Battle Quits, Black Mayor Seated

Shortly after six years of wrestling, with little success, to improve conditions in the city, Mayor Battle decided to move to a more comfortable and prestigious seat as a county judge, following in

Politics and Prejudice

the footsteps of another ex-mayor, Gorbey. His successor in this latest game of political chess was Mrs. Willie Mae James Leake, the city's first Black—and female—mayor. She had moved nimbly through the system before reaching this crowning position by way of some shrewd alliances and appointments.

She was once an aide to undertaker Lewis M. Hunt (a Ninth Ward political boss) and was a former member of the school board on which Hunt once served. After resigning that position, she served as city treasurer and tax collector. Her next move was as secretary to then-mayor Nacrelli, and later Battle. In addition to her political responsibilities, she served on church and civic committees, and with her husband, Willie, co-owned the Leake Funeral Home.

As an ex-council member who was appointed the new mayor, Mrs. Leake soon began surrounding herself with a personal team of Blacks, some of whom had minor posts in prior administrations, including John Nails, city solicitor, and Leon Bean, planning chief. Significantly, her new police chief was Lawrence Crews who had come up through local schools as well as the ranks of his department.

Otherwise, anyone trying to move into this inner circle experienced only frustration or indifference inside both the racial and political fence. Two examples of this were Bill Riley, a young progressive

Mayor Willie Mae Leake.

city policeman, and the Rev. Andrew T. Holtz, Jr., a city-bred clergyman, who at different times sought seats on city council. Riley, a son-in-law of veteran patrolman Leroy Richardson (whose father was a Ninth Ward politico) sought to field an independent councilmanic ticket in 1983 to challenge the Battle faction.[15] One of his running mates was the Rev. Johnny Monroe, the Presbyterian minister named "Man of the Year" in 1978 by the Negro Women's Business and Professional Club. However, before Riley could get up any steam for his campaign, almost the entire 134 names on his nominating petition list were invalidated. Mayor Battle contended that fifty-one of the signers were unregistered, and that another thirty names carried addresses unlisted in county registration records. Common Pleas Judge Howard F. Reed, a War Board appointee, agreed with Mayor Battle.[16]

Young Rev. Holtz, pastor of Murphy AME Church, tossed his hat into the same ring in the spring of 1987, vying for a council seat only to go down in defeat. Commenting on the event, the Rev. Gilbert Caldwell, pastor of St. Daniel's Methodist Church and former associate general secretary of the Methodist Church on Race and Religion, afterwards wrote:

"During the campaign on election day, many of us felt that there were some persons who were so angered or threatened by his candidacy that they resorted to tactics unworthy of our Christian democratic process. It is my hope that all of the political leaders of every party in Chester will recognize and remember that government that is not of, for and by the people does not serve any of the people at all. The political party in power does not seem to encourage creative, independent involvement and debate."[17]

On Mayor Leake's winning ticket for her first full four-year term were several more Blacks, obviously endorsed by the real power brokers. Stephen McKeller, a Streets Improvement assistant, took the council seat vacated earlier by the forced resignation, due to a personal scandal, of Councilman Jimmy Sharpe. (Leo S. Holmes, the first Black councilman, had served as the interim appointee.) William L. Brown, Jr., the regional justice since 1979, could be considered a part of the increasing Black administration team. Others included the Rev. William "Rocky" Brown III as controller;

Politics and Prejudice

Above: David Womack. Right: Rev. William Brown III.

and Peggy Charleston, one-time housing project manager, who won her third 4-year term as city clerk. Ms. Charleston was also a Chester-Upland School Board member.

Adding to the crime and welfare problems, the city had the highest rate of teen-age pregnancy in the state, boosted by the fact that 26 percent of births in 1984 were to mothers under twenty years of age.[18] The state Department of Education, aware of the situation and its deleterious effect on student accomplishments, made $1.3 million available for schools to cope with such problems. Surprisingly, the Chester-Upland School District did not receive any of the funds. Explaining the reason for his district's failure to file applications for any of the funds, Superintendent Harold Smith said, "We were busy with other things, concentrating on competency tests, and evaluations at the high school."[19]

For some publicly unexplained cause, the newness and excitement of the ultra-modern high school offering a wide variety of subjects and training was beginning to wear thin, judging from the gradual decline in both enrollment and graduations at the periods when the total number of Black families were increasing. A survey in August, 1982 showed an alarming percentage of absentee rates among Chester High students: 25% for freshmen, 20% for sophomores and juniors, and 21% for seniors.[20] In the June, 1985 graduating class, only 365 received diplomas—a striking contrast to the 480 Blacks alone in the 1974 class, the first from the new school. As further evidence of student decline, only 323 graduated from the 1988-89 school year[21] according to the state Board of Education, which also noted that dropouts from Chester High at that period totaled 242, the highest number among Delaware County high schools.[22]

Role Models Who Made Good

If some young persons did decide to forsake school and education due to the seeming bleakness of career possibilities, there were at least a couple of former Chesterites whose stars were currently soaring high over the national horizon. The two potential role models were Dr. Lenora Branch Fulani, a one-time presidential candidate; and Dr. Howard Dodson, chief of the nation's best-known library on the Black Experience. Both managed to overcome stifling odds in their home town.

Ms. Fulani, daughter of Pearl Branch, and winner of an amateur singing contest, became bitter and left town after her father died because ambulances refused to transport him to a hospital, claiming fear of entering Black neighborhoods. "I was taught in the sixth grade that all men were created equal," she said later, "but that was a bunch of hogwash."

Dr. Lenora Fulani. Photograph courtesy of AroundHarlem.com.

Politics and Prejudice

She later graduated from Hofstra and Columbia universities and became active in New York civic and political circles. As a candidate for the New Alliance Party in the 1988 presidential election, she placed fourth in the final polls, beating out such well-known candidates as Eugene McCarthy and Lyndon LaRouch. She later served as director of a community clinic for the Institute of Social Therapy and Research in New York City.

Dodson, a 1954 Chester High graduate, became an employee at the U. S. Post Office in Chester, where he once faced serious charges in connection with his job. Thirty years later, with additional education and experience to his credit, Dodson became chief of the Schomburg Center for Research in Black Culture in New York City. In that post he assumed authority for the agency's activities, including library operations, personnel development and public programs. His education included studies at West Chester State, Villanova, UCLA and University of California at Berkeley. As proof of the "local boy makes good", Widener University bestowed upon him in 1987 an honorary Doctorate of Humane Letters.

Over the years, of course, others forsook the town seeking to accomplish goals not considered readily available here, yet the achievements of these two role models provided current news for the eyes of the present generation. Almost simultaneously, hundreds of ex-Chesterites returned briefly in August, 1988 to attend a gala three-day reunion for students of the Frederick Douglass Junior High, which closed its doors permanently earlier in the decade. All the participants were obviously thrilled to meet old friends and reminisce over bygone days, and to cite memorials to deceased instructors.

That generation acquainted with some of the Douglass alumni, incidentally, may never have been aware of a handful of surviving individuals—appropriate role models, also—who kept up the battle for equality since the later Depression days. One in particular was George T. Raymond who graduated from Chester High School a year after Douglass School opened. One of the groups of youths closely identified with local churches, "Y" programs and similar activities, he succeed to the NAACP presidency in the early 1940s and served in that capacity continually for nearly three

Chapter 10

decades afterwards. Sometimes single-handedly, he investigated any citizen's complaint of police illegal tactics, public accommodations or job discrimination. The cases he was unable to resolve were settled in court.

A long-time occupant of the Lamokin Housing Project, the uncompromising Raymond, despite needed expenses for a growing family, was forced to earn his wages as a laborer or janitor. Strongly opposed to the political machine, nonetheless he remained on civil terms with its Black lieutenants.

If anyone expected this man to fit the classic identity of a charismatic leader, they would be sorely mistaken. First of all, he stuttered terribly, and was barely five feet tall. Few acquaintances expected him to be on time for a meeting. He often paused along the way for conversations with folks, listening to civic complaints or persuading others to join the NAACP. Eventually, he persuaded some of the conservative element to come aboard, assigning responsible positions to them.

Only after a hard-fought but successful battle to purchase a home in suburbia did he give up his Chester residence. Yet, still NAACP head, he served as a spark plug in the 1964 school desegregation campaign, just as he had in 1946. Since his retirement, an annual "George T. Raymond Achievement Award," in his honor, has been presented to a person who, during the preceding year, most typified his Herculean efforts in the field of civil and human rights.

Rising over the horizon during the subsequent generation of Raymond's epoch came William "Billy" Brown, Jr., who ultimately survived the political minefield while distinguishing himself in the realms of public service for the town's Blacks. The son of Ethel Brown, a leader (along with Raymond and others) in the school reform movement that began at the old Watts School where "Billy" was a second-grade pupil, he graduated from Chester High in 1952. After earning a B.A. degree at Cheyney State University, he became a teacher and later assistant principal in the local school district. Extending his schooling, he attendee Villanova Graduate School for a major in educational administration afterwards becoming director of the Greater Chester Movement's Day Care

Center for Handicapped Children.

To many, his crowning achievement was his 1979 appointment—and successive elected terms—as the first Black to hold the regional justice office in Chester.

Brown's organization memberships included the Alpha Phi Alpha Fraternity, J. Wesley Parker Phalanx Fraternity, John A. Watts Elks Lodge, Eastern Light Lodge #46 of the Masons, Delaware County Justice Association, Delaware County Republican Council, the Holy City Civic Association and Calvary Baptist Church. Among his personal citations were the Chester School District's Distinguished Service Award, the John A. Watts Elks Lodge Outstanding Service Award, The Chester Community Humanitarian Award and Black Expo Political Achievement Award.

Tragically, his meteoric rise came to an end when he died at the relatively young age of fifty-six in October, 1990.[23] In his obituary he was described as a "beloved and much-honored lifelong resident." Cognizant of his political and civic strength, there were those who suspected Brown could or would sever his political ties to command an independent reform movement among Blacks.

Unfortunately, the town, which some returnees for the Douglass Junior High reunion termed "depressing," could not provide adequate facilities to accommodate the hundreds of "old grads." Those not rooming with relatives had to register at various county motels. Their reception was held at the Sun Center in nearby Feltonville, and the closing Sunday services were conducted in the First Pentecostal Church (the former Columbus Center) on Pusey near Third Street, the only building in the area spacious enough for the occasion.

On the subject of public gatherings, thousands of Black citizens were never cramped for space during two particular annual celebrations—the Mother's Day parade and ceremonies, and the participants in the NAACP picnic in September at the city park in south Chester. The local Elks generally sponsored the Mother's Day events which drew delegations of fraternal groups and youth marching clubs from cities as far away as Coatesville and Downingtown.

Chapter 10

William Brown, Jr.

In spite of the large minority group population, a relative few public self-help and character-molding programs for teenagers and adolescents were available in the hard-pressed eighties. One of the most significant institutions, the West End YMCA operation, which had finally come into being after more than a decade of disappointments to the community, had to terminate its activities in early 1981.[24] The Pew family, which originally helped finance the building, donated $55,000 in the final months, all attempts to raise adequate funds having failed. Max Winston and the Rev. Johnnie Monroe, regular "Y" boosters, charged that local citizens had not been sufficiently warned of the program's serious financial plight even before the local depression set in.[25] The YM complex was eventually purchased by Murphy AME Church, whose edifice sits across the street. It was renamed the Chester Family Center, adding one more of the programs being sponsored by denominational churches and volunteer groups.

On the opposite side of town, where there were comparatively smaller neighborhoods of Hispanics and Blacks, and where there remained century-old stone churches left in fair condition by well-heeled congregations, other programs also carried on for the less fortunate. The United Methodist Church at Seventh and Madison Streets, renamed Wesley House, served as a temporary shelter, furnishing counseling, clothing and food. A few blocks away,

157

in the old Presbyterian Church building, renamed the Eastside Ministries, Widener College students, led by David Womack, conducted volunteer services and supervised tutorial lessons for 8- to 13-year-old children. Swarthmore College students began working on a five-year, $125,000 grant from Scott Paper Company designed to help with inner-city housing rehabilitation and the organization of a debate club at Chester High School.

For those whose interest was inclined towards things artistic, the Alfred O. Deshong Memorial Arts and Cultural Center, located on Edgmont Avenue, sponsored year-round art exhibits, concerts, drama and education activities. Anzer Kirkland, a Cheyney graduate, founded and led the Chester Fine Arts Center-East prior to his appointment as director of the Deshong project.[26]

Organizations dealing with health problems included the AIDS Coalition, Inc., DARE (Drug Abuse Resistance Education), CAN (Church Against Narcotics) and several public clinics. AIDS Coalition was a nonprofit, community-based organization committed to releasing information to the public and providing supportive measures for persons infected with the virus. It had a board of directors, an executive and a staff that included volunteers. The DARE organization was an affiliate of the nationwide movement concentrating on teaching school children to resist pressure to experiment with drugs and alcohol. The CAN project originated in Calvary Baptist Church with its pastor, the Rev. Kirk Jones. Other local churches also participated.

If Black hearts swelled with pride, now that several of their own, especially the mayor, finally held important policy-making positions, some of the more observant citizens perhaps realized that "things aren't always what they seem," as one veteran city-watcher wryly observed.

It was unfortunate for hopeful citizens that those prestigious municipal seats came about almost simultaneously with the deterioration of the area's economy, the dangerous increase in drug and crime activity, plus the increase in welfare dependency. Quite similar to other cities where Blacks had migrated in large numbers seeking employment in wartime, now the slumping industries, followed by fearful whites, had taken their taxable

Chapter 10

resources to other climes.

Moreover, most of the Blacks sitting in the pecking order reached there bereft of any practical experience or training in economics, which was badly needed to help lift the city from its socioeconomic doldrums. To make matters worse, Mayor Leake, despite being fairly well-grounded in the rudiments of local politics, had to suffer constant interference from ex-mayor Nacrelli who was forbidden by the court to hold public office until 1992. From all appearances, Nacrelli was making his presence felt heavily in numerous municipal and political matters. His reputed stranglehold over important city business seemed more public than the shadowy manipulations of the late John McClure. He met frequently with members of both the council and the school board, and sat several times in important meetings claiming to represent the council.[27]

Testifying before the Pennsylvania Crime Commission investigating crime and corruption in Chester, one witness said, ". . . the Mayor wants to move Nacrelli out, but she will not . . . I don't know whether it's because he was the one that brought her up the political ladder or what, but she has some kind of allegiance with him."[28]

The Crime Commission, taking cognizance of Nacrelli negotiating an important contract with Westinghouse Electric on behalf of the city, concluded, "The perception that government must rely upon or call upon convicted racketeers to mediate disputes in an industry historically tainted with organized crime involvement, serves no other end but to suggest to citizens of Chester that racketeers still decide public policy issues in the city of Chester."

Asked about Nacrelli's continued power in the city, his attorney Arthur Levy, answered, "Mr. Nacrelli only has as much power as the people in Chester allow him to have. And that is democracy."[29] Surely, Levy, a veteran in his profession, was aware that his client was not chosen for any public office in the latest democratically run election.

Responding more objectively to the controversy, James Manning, Crime Commission vice-chairman, also a Republican, called Chester "a classic case of government at its worst."[29]

FIRST BLACK WOMAN APPOINTED MAYOR
Bibliography

1. *Philadelphia Tribune*, February 5, 1982.

2. *Philadelphia Inquirer*, March 3, 1988.

3. *Delaware County Daily Times*, July 21, 1982.

4. Ibid, February 28, 1989. *Inquirer*, March 3, 1989.

5. *New York Times*, January 9, 1981.

6. *City-County Data Book*, U.S. Census, 1983.

7. *Philadelphia Tribune*, February 5, 1982.

8. *City-County Data Book*, U.S. Census, 1983.

9. *Delaware County Daily Times*, August 2, 1982.

10. Uniform Crime Reports, U.S. Department of Justice.

11. *Philadelphia Inquirer*, September 29, 1989.

12. *Delaware County Daily Times*, May 30, 1990.

13. Ibid, October 10, 1983.

14. Ibid, May 4, 1985.

15. Ibid, July 20, 1983.

16. Ibid, July 23, 1983.

17. Ibid, July 9, 1987.

18. *City-County Data Book*, U.S. Census, 1988.

19. *Delaware County Daily Times*, September 15, 1985.

20. Ibid, August 26, 1982.

21. Public School Dropout Rate, 1988-89, Pennsylvania Department of Education, Harrisburg.

22. Ibid.

23. *Delaware County Daily Times*, October 24, 1990.

24. Ibid, July 20, 1981.

Chapter 10

25. Ibid, November 2, 1982.

26. Chester Educational Task Force, Vol. 1, No. 2.

27. *Delaware County Daily Times*, February 28, 1989.

28. *Philadelphia Inquirer*, March 2, 1989.

29. Ibid.

EPILOGUE

Chester is a microcosm of many municipalities of various sizes across the nation; the one important exception is that it is among the oldest. Unfortunately it allowed itself to develop hardening of the arteries, socioeconomically speaking, through constant neglect in not properly exercising its body politic. Over the years, Pennsylvania's senior city ultimately suffered through the same phases as did other cities—Black and white migrations, interracial unrest, wartime prosperities, civil-rights commotion, industrial-business uncertainties. Through it all, Blacks were kept in subservient roles so much that some jokingly referred to the city as "McClure's Plantation." However, if that facetious analogy would advance a step further, the wealthy Pews could be termed the masters and John J. McClure, their wily overseer. Black strawbosses were customarily appointed to keep the subjects in line.

Jokes aside, Blacks somehow missed one of their first opportunities during the Second World War to shake off those political shackles. That particular instance occurred when some sixty men whose backgrounds included religion, business, sports, labor and education banded together for the formation of the city's first Black YMCA. Virtually all the organization members—independent, influential individuals in some specific community agency or project—consequently enjoyed a sizable degree of grass-roots constituency.

After the goal was met, a suggestion to form a permanent reform group was floated. Dick Thomas, the ex-college grid star with an advanced business-finance education and a member of a financially well-off family, was deemed to possess the potential to assume the leadership mantle. He, however, demonstrated no interest in the role. Another school of thought saw any reform efforts fail because wartime migrants, many with college backgrounds, showed little or no concern with local civic problems. Some residents, in direct contrast, were traditionally leery of accepting newcomers into their confidences.

EPILOGUE

These attitudes were fairly well altered in the subsequent generation when a total stranger, Stanley L. Branche, burst upon the scene and formed his "Committee For Freedom Now" a civilian army, nearly one-half of which was youthful followers, to challenge the system that kept Blacks relegated to second-class citizenship for years. Most of his additional forces consisted of former "baby boomers," now the parents of the younger shock troops. Many of the latter group no doubt had been inspired by their elders' partial victories in the school protest activities of the mid-1940s. This new movement also drew in a small cadre of new, young professionals along with the NAACP which was finally strengthened by some of the more conservative elements that previously had kept their distance from the chapter's leadership.

When the dust of the long, drawn-out battle had finally cleared, the Black population, having virtually doubled, began receiving a modicum of civic and political consideration—that is, as much as the bosses (the War Board) would permit under their own terms. Even so, the machine operatives maintained their usual control. Whatever outsiders may think, locals can take little direct credit for the gradual appearance of members of their race in public offices, as practically every one of those officeholders had been selected by GOP leaders. The king-makers indeed were obviously certain a Black could not win a city-wide office, given the long-existing anti-Black atmosphere for which they themselves were largely responsible. Noticeably, these appointments and subsequent elections began in the mid-1960s when the white population was becoming the minority group. During that period of riots and picketing, the increasingly volatile Black revolutionaries seemingly held the Sword of Damocles in their hands.

Judging from current events, there looms the possibility of the local political system continuing to operate in the same mode for years to come. Certain Black officials, for example, tolerated the unauthorized meetings of the convicted ex-mayor with members of both the city council and school board, and also his negotiation of a city contract with a private firm. Peggy Charleston, who held the dual posts of city clerk and school board member, once contended the former mayor's acceptance of a $20,000 bribe that sent him to prison was no more than the amount of the annual salary of an average citizen.[1]

Although it is no necessary reflection on their personal calibre or reputation, the estimated 400-500 schoolteachers and other personnel most generally would favor their GOP sponsors during city elections. The same could be expected of the similar number of municipal workers. However, in regard to teachers (unfortunately too few are males), many find themselves giving support to a political operation often closing its eyes on unethical and/or illegal manipulations.

The gradual seating of Blacks in strategic municipal positions also came about as the economy hit rock bottom, exacerbating problems of unemployment, welfare, crimes, etc. As similar situations have occurred in numerous cities across the nation, several studies have been undertaken on such matters. Many of the findings list possible pitfalls as well the positive contributions that face newcomer Black officials. Some could be applicable to Chester:

1. They must learn to bargain with the private sector and other public officials with access to far greater revenue.

2. Due to political and economic constraints, they often face significant limitations on freedom to maneuver.

3. Black mayors are generally saddled with declining employment and revenue bases.

4. Police harassment and unnecessary use of force generally decline when Blacks are appointed to higher positions in law enforcement departments.[2]

In the final analysis, even if and when more Blacks become elected to important municipal posts, there are no leadpipe assurances that worthwhile reforms will come about, as some observers have opined. Clarence Page, a Chicago columnist, for instance, wrote on the subject of Black mayors, "Political victories less economic gains are hollow victories."[3] Extended, it doubtlessly means that until the infrastructures of Black communities are rebuilt to begin eliminating the problems of crime, educational underachievement, teen-age pregnancy and welfare dependency, there can be little or no relief in such cities.

The state of any organized crime situation in prior times has been best uncovered and prosecuted through the combination of federal and state jurisdictions. The Pennsylvania Crime Commission, responsible for exposing the policy syndicate a decade earlier, began again in the mid-1980s to investigate suspected criminal activities of a Philadelphia Mafia[4] faction aiming to team up with small-time drug merchants in Chester where street trafficking in drugs continues to plague the narcotics squads.

The city's difficult task of coping with the drug situation, especially as it involves youth, was scheduled to receive some welcome relief. A $50 million facility, a gift from the state, would house some six hundred young prisoners guilty of drug and alcohol offenses. "It will be a rehabilitative type, not maximum security," Mayor Leake explained.[5]

The economy was expected to get a relatively fair boost, according to the mayor, who added that the contemplated project would provide approximately three hundred jobs, including staff and supervisors. "I hope most of the positions will go to Chester people," she stated, evidently expressing concerns that this latest construction undertaking would make local hiring one of its priorities. Current with her observations was the construction of the County Resource Recovery Center at the foot of Highland Avenue. During that period when the city jobless rate was at record high, numerous workers on the construction companies' payrolls hailed from New York, New Jersey, Philadelphia and other parts of Delaware County.

The city's jobless rate remained virtually stagnant in the eighties while some large construction works were in progress, and contractors apparently had a sizable pool of local construction workers which they could tap. For example, approximately twenty-two hundred Black machine operators, fabricators, transportation workers and other semiskilled persons were available in Chester, according to the "Occupation and Class of Employable Persons" listed by the 1980 U.S. Census.[6] Of course, should municipal authorities fail to insist on stipulating equal opportunity provisos in such contracts, out-of-town companies would have free rein in their selection of work crews.

Convenient availability of improved educational pursuits through secondary, vocational schools and colleges offer fairly hopeful signs to aid in helping to pull the populace out of its economic doldrums. Employment opportunities for qualified workers would also await such fortunate persons in other parts of the county, as well as in Philadelphia, a thirty-minute ride northward.

When days seem darkest for a predominantly Black community, perhaps it could look to the two important institutions that helped encourage and sustain them through the early days of the century—their churches and newspapers.

Their churches, of course, are still increasing rapidly, some directing their approaches towards influencing the secular lives of citizens. More white congregations in recent years have also become involved in serving the underprivileged minorities. Equally important are the efforts of their main-line denominations, such as the Presbyterians, Baptists, Methodists, plus Quakers, in helping sponsor affordable housing in Black neighborhoods. Others have crusaded for Black rights to purchase homes in so-called white communities. Some of the white clergy whose congregations have abandoned their edifices for new county locations have returned to join civil rights protest activities, aware of the concerns and aspirations of those Christian Blacks who continue to struggle for decent livelihoods in the ghettoes.

Many of these Black citizens, recent migrants from rural areas, poor and isolated, have joined the growing number of small, storefront Pentecostal churches that traditionally stress the spiritual, believing that prayer rather than medicine and physicians can heal their physical ailments. Yet, overall, obviously due to the existing philosophical cleavage, they and the larger Black denominations have seldom combined their resources to fight against bias, civic neglect and public corruption.

There evidently has existed among the "brain-trust" of the good folks of the larger Black churches the notion that the combined

EPILOGUE

memberships of all their churches could possibly effect a successful voting bloc strong enough to elect independent-minded persons to public offices. That general idea was attempted—and failed—in the not-too-distant past when two young ministers, the Reverends Johnny Monroe (Presbyterian) and Andrew Holtz (AME) campaigned for city council seats on two distinct occasions. During several past decades, it may be recalled, there were several instances when pastors became outspoken on political matters only to have their tenures suddenly abbreviated. At the other end of the spectrum, two of them, the Reverends Daniel A. Scott, of Bethany Baptist, and J. Pius Barbour, of Calvary Baptist, were diplomatic enough to survive forty-year tenures while contributing immensely to community reform. Interestingly, neither aspired for political recognition, yet both utilized their prestige to back a few of their members for non-elective jobs.

During the times when Black-owned newspapers are regaining recognition as significant instruments of public awareness and information for their readers, Chester is unfortunate to not have such an important monitor at its disposal. Years back when the short-lived *Crusader* weekly newspaper campaigned aggressively for racial equality, its primary readership was centered in south Chester where problems were seen and felt most acutely. Those who were not regular subscribers could rely on getting their latest news either "over-the-back-fence" or in barber shops or beauty salons. Now that Blacks are gradually scattering far outside the south Chester environs, the need is greater for some type of media targeting such potential readers. Neither the *Delaware County Times*, now located in the county, nor Philadelphia papers, including the *Tribune*, the nation's oldest race-owned publication, can substitute for a locally owned, independent Black newspaper.

In the wake of the sixties civic rebellion, the state and conscious-stricken industrialists combined a small portion of their resources to launch a rejuvenation movement particularly to appease uprising Blacks, accumulating a minimum of success. The future may now lie in the hands and hearts of the city's majority—the estimated 65 percent Blacks. Many of these residents comprise the second and third generations of those combat-hardened citizens that braved the clubs, police dogs, jail, injury and often ridicule in those fairly victorious marches of the forties and twenty years later.

Colored, Negro, Black, Afro-American—whatever the current and future generations choose to call themselves, they are the minorities that finally grew into the majority. Ordinarily, a "majority" represents strength in numbers.

No well-meaning American citizen should fail to realize the folly of living in a city of racial exclusiveness, whether among its residences or its policy-makers. Every ethnic group nevertheless must nurture its self-respect and pride, though not at the expense of another. One prominent clergyman, a former resident, offered this advice:

"...We live together in the same city as members of all races, yet we do not have enough authentic sharing of our different histories and experiences. We do not understand how important it is for all of us to participate in decision-making and power-sharing. The time for token presence and plantation mentality ought to be gone. The future of Chester is dependent upon leadership of strong persons of every race... Chester can be a model of authentic, productive, multi-racial community if we dare to look to the future and stop holding to the past."[7]

EPILOGUE Bibliography

1. *Delaware County Daily Times*, February 28, 1989.

2. *Blacks and American Society* (National Academy Press, 1989), p. 251.

3. Clarence Page, *Merge Magazine*, June, 1990.

4. *Delaware County Daily Times*, February 28, 1989.

5. *Philadelphia Inquirer*, May 1, 1990.

6. *City-County Data Book*, U.S. Department of Commerce, U.S. Census, 1980.

7. Gilbert H. Caldwell, *Race, Religion and Reconstruction* (Simon Publishing Co., 1989), p. 94.

APPENDIX

DELAWARE COUNTY POPULATION

Year	White	Colored
1790	9,144	289
1800	12,157	645
1810	13,912	822
1820	13,701	1,108
1830	16,062	1,258
1840	18,458	1,333
1850	23,122	1,557
1860	28,948	1,649
1870	36,659	2,744
1880	51,487	4,612
1890	67,684	6,965

Source: U.S. Census.

CHESTER (PA.) POPULATION

Year	Total	Blacks
1900	33,988	3,398
1910	39,000	6,100
1920	58,760	7,277
1930	59,164	9,038
1940	59,285	10,183
1950	66,039	13,865
1960	63,658	21,274
1970	56,331	25,904
1980	45,794	27,000
1990	41,856	27,260
2000	36,854	27,897

Source: U.S. Census and City (updated to 2000 for this edition).

Reasons for Coming to Chester as an Adult Heads of Households, by Race Selected Census Tracts, City of Chester, 1967

	Total		White		Nonwhite	
	Number	%	Number	%	Number	%
Seek employment	42	12.1	10	7.9	32	14.5
Definite job offer	37	10.6	19	15.1	18	8.1
Live with family or relatives	43	12.4	21	16.7	22	10
Housing available	7	2	5	4	2	0.9
Educational opportunities	3	0.9	1	0.8	2	0.9
Combination of employment, housing, and family ties	161	46.4	44	34.9	117	52.9
Other N.E.C.	11	3.2	7	5.5	4	1.8
Not reported	43	12.4	19	15.1	24	10
	347	100	126	100	221	100

Source: Sample Survey Data. "Barriers To Employment Growth In A Depressed Area," unpublished thesis by John T. Meli, Widener College, 1972.

APPENDIX

1987-88 DROPOUT RATE, CHESTER-UPLAND SCHOOLS

Chester-Upland District	Enrollments Grades 7-12	Dropouts			Dropout Rate	Dropout Rate, 2006
		Male	Female	Total		
Chester High School*	1,697	164	78	242	14.26	12.7
Main Street School	137	2	1	3	2.19	8.0
Pulaski Middle School	281	7	4	11	3.91	-
Showalter Middle School	324	2	2	4	1.23	6.1
Smedley Middle School	352	0	5	5	1.42	22.3
Total	2,791	175	90	265	9.49	12.1

*Chester High School had highest dropout rate among the county's 15 districts' high schools. Source: Pennsylvania Department of Education (2006 data added for this edition).

STUDENT STATISTICS FOR THREE LARGEST DELAWARE COUNTY SCHOOL DISTRICTS

School District	Enrollments			Schools (Total)	Grads (1988)	College	Other
	Total	Elementary	Secondary				
Chester-Upland	7,119	4,547	2,572	11	323	81	3
Haverford Township	4,466	2,455	2,011	7	402	125	8
Ridley	4,294	2,287	2,007	9	399	184	36

Index

A

Africa, Mary and Moe 149
Afro-American (newspaper) 43
AIDS Coalition, Inc. 158
Alfred O. Deshong Memorial Arts and Cultural Center 158
Allen Endeavor 47
Andrews, Frank 93, 97
Apollo Theater 42, 85
Association of Negroes in American Industry 69
Atlantic Refining Co. 77
Atlantic Steel Co. 125
August Quarterly, 111

B

Baldwin Locomotive 70, 77
Banana Alley 19
Banneker Plaza 140
Baptist Training Union 47
Barbour, Rev. J. Pious 50, 71, 94, 117, 167
Battle, Mayor Joseph H. 144, 149
Bean, Leon 150
Bennett Home for Negro Girls 26, 89
Bennett, R. L. Terrace Homes 107, 148
Benn Theater 39
Berry, Oakley 76, 91
Bethel Court 20, 37, 92, 107
Bloom, Leah 49
Blow, Beverly 59
Bobo, D. Nelson 48, 71
Boeing Aircraft 125
Bond, Cecil 47, 65, 93, 136
Bond, Frinjella 93, 96, 97, 136
Bouldin, Alex 41
Bowen, Leamon 65
Branche, Stanley 116, 124, 130, 163
Brown, Catherine 62

Index

Brown, Ethel 93, 97, 136, 137
Brown, William III 137, 151
Brown, William Jr. 137, 151, 155
Bryant, Ella 141
Bryn Mawr College 119
Burley, Charley 41

C

Cameron, Thomas E. 48
Campbell, Chauncey L. 84
CAN (Church Against Narcotics) 158
Carter, Att'y Robert L. 122
Central Boys Club 65, 73
Chadwick, E. Wallace 88
Charleston, Peggy 152, 163
Chester Businessmen's Association 122
Chester churches
  Asbury AME 17
  Bethany Baptist 34, 45
  Calvary Baptist Church 26, 115
  Fifth Presbyterian (also T. M. Thomas) 45
  First Pentecostal 111, 156
  Murphy AME 48, 111
  Providence Baptist 26
  Range's Temple 54, 111
  Shiloh Baptist 111
  Spencer (Welsh Street) Union AME 107, 111
  St. Daniel's Methodist 17, 27, 95
  St. Hedwig's Catholic 41
  St. John's AUMP 18, 111
  St. Luke's Christian Methodist 112
Chester Family Center 157
Chester Fine Arts Center-East 158
Chester Housing Authority 74, 107, 132, 137
Chester Human Relations Committee 117
Chester Industrial School 20
Chester Redevelopment Authority 107, 129
Chester School Board 31, 92
Chester Times (newspaper) 43

Chester Township 99, 108
Chester-Upland School Board 135, 152
Chester Water Company 36, 69, 90
Cheyney State College 22, 39, 104
Civil War 17
Colder, Katie 18
Columbus Center 156
Comets A. C. 40
Committee for Freedom Now 116, 163
Commodore Barry Bridge 132, 138, 147
Community United Methodist Church 111
Congress of Racial Equality (CORE) 121
"Cool Breeze" 39
Cooper, Ralph 40
Crews, Lawrence 150
Crews, Ollie 78
Crozer, J. Lewis, Library 141
Crozer Theological Seminary 50
Crump, Ed 29
Crusader (newspaper) 83, 96, 99, 167
Curley, James 29

D

DARE (Drug Abuse Resistance Education) 158
Davis, "Slats" 39
Dawson, Herman 117
Day Company, Joseph 75
Delaware County Black Policemen's Association 133
Delaware County Children's College 120
Delaware County Community College 104
Delaware County Republican Council 156
Delaware County Resource Recovery Center 165
Delaware County Times 167
Delaware River 15, 147
Delaware, State of 16
Dewey, James 88
Dewitt, Robert 122
Dilworth, Richardson 105
Dodson, Howard 153

Index

Dougherty, Jimmy 41
Drew, T. N. 20
Drexel Hill 110
Driggins, John 104
Dunbar A. C. 64
Dunbar Literary Society 49
Durnell, Catherine 84
Dutch West Indies Company 15

E

Earle, Gov. George 37
East Side Ministries 158
Educational Equality League 95, 97
Elks Lodge 22, 26, 147
Engineering, Science and Management War Training Program 67
Epworth League 47
Ethel Waters Park 132
Excelsior Village 141
Eyre, Mayor Joseph 119

F

Fairgrounds Housing Project 77
Fairgrounds Residents Assoc. 94
Farmer, James 121
Fauset, Crystal Bird 37
Federal Works Administration 73
Floyd family 65
Fontaine, Donald 54
Fontaine, Herman 133, 134
Fontaine, Otto 135
Fontaine, William 135
Fordham, Jefferson 122
Ford Motor Co. 70, 125
Franklin, Jack 121
Freeman, Bea 40
Fritz, Beulah 75
Fritz, F. Herman 95

Froggy Bottom 20
Fry, Ed 30, 111
Fulani, Dr. Lenora 153

G

Galamison, Rev. Milton 45
Garnett, Henry H. 23
Gethers, Noah 54, 65
Girard College 124
Girl Scouts 45
Godfrey, George 41
Goode, Wilson 140
Gorbey, James H. 129
Gorbey, John 132
Gouley, Att'y Henry 91, 95
Graham, Theodore (Ted) 43, 65
Grand United Order of True Believers 22
Grasty, Edward 99
Grasty, James 39, 59, 98
Grasty, William 99
Gra-Y club 54, 69
Greater Chester Movement 123, 125, 155
Green, Casper H. 32, 50
Green, Jeremiah Sr. 32
Green, Leanna 33
Green, Millicent 33
Green, Talbot 65
Gregory, Dick 118
Griffin, Levi 76

H

Hague, Frank 29
Handy, Ed 76
Handy, "Happy" 39
Hardy, Larney M. 82, 87, 96
Harper, Wilson 48, 84, 108
Harris, Commodore, Jr. 133
Harris, Roscoe 55

Index

Harris, William, Sr. 46
Henderson, Dr. W. H. 71, 96
Henderson, J. H. 82
Henry, Florence 21
Henry, Mrs. W. A. 21
Henson Hi-Y club 49, 54
Hewet, Rev. Clayton 119
Hill, Leon J. 59
Holland, Jerome (Brud) 69
Hollingsworth, Anna 97
Holmes, Leo S. 124, 134, 151
Holt, Bill 46
Holtz, Rev. Andrew, Jr. 151, 167
Hoopes, William 134
HUD 139
Hunt, Alex 65, 135
Hunt, Joseph S. 75, 82, 84
Hunt, Lewis M., Jr. 45, 97
Hunt, Lewis M., Sr. 27, 31, 32, 51, 59, 106
Hunt, Norman 84
Hunt, Palmer 129

I

Independent Civic League 44, 91, 94
Irish Alley 19

J

Jackson, Stan 40
Jacobs, General 79
Jaffee, Joseph X. 122
Johnson, Eugene 48, 136
Johnson, Reginald 68
Jones, London B. 65
Jones, Rev. Kirk 158

K

Kelly, Francis X. 105
Kerns, J. Harvey 89

177

"Kid Kanky" 39
Kieffer, Dewey 76
King Homes, Martin Luther 52, 138
King, Martin Luther, Jr. 51, 115
Kinlaw, Robert 133
Kirkland, Anzer 158
Kiwanis Club 144
Knights of Pythias Lodge 22
Ku Klux Klan 96
Kyle, Rev. Dwight V. 48

L

Lamokin Village housing project 54, 75, 108
Lang, George 66
Larkin, Charles "Pard" 64
Laws, Catherine (see also Brown) 120
Laws, Herman 44, 48, 63, 67
Laws, Theodore (Ted) 92, 105
Leake, Mayor Willie Mae James 150, 159, 165
Levy, Arthur 159
Lewis, Floyd 134
Lewis, Isiah 48, 82
Lewis, John 121
Liberia Alley 20
Lincoln University 22, 39
Link, Rev. J. L. 49
Logan, Floyd 95
Long Bottom Gut 19
Long, Charles 119, 123
Loper, Margaret 65

M

Mack, Will 21
Mafia 165
Mailman, Morris 42, 87
Malcolm X 118
Manning, James 159
Margoline, Matthew 42, 52, 85

Market Street Massacre 92, 104
Maryland, State of 16, 23
Masonic Lodges 22, 147
McCabe, Thomas B. 123
McCaffrey housing project 75
McClure, John 25, 29, 36, 51, 69, 88, 106, 114, 121, 129, 144
McDonald, Lonnie 54
McDowell, William 25
McKeller, Stephen 151
McKinney, Nina Mae 40
McLinn, Angela 92
Meli, John T. 127
Merrick, Raleigh 141
Miah, Leroy 133
Miller, Dr. Thomas M. 46
Miller, Jack 46
Miller's Drug Store 41
Ming, Rev. Donald 117
Mitchell, Clarence 68
Mitchell, George 74
Moll, Clarence 104, 123
Money, Helen 65
Monroe, Rev. Johnny 151, 157, 167
Moore, Dorothy 65
Moore, Jimmy 41
Moore, "Red" 39
Moore, Rev. Leon S. 49
Moore, Rev. Noah 50
Morgan State College 39
Morris, Jack 39
Moses, Ethel 40
Mother's Day Festival 156
MOVE 149
Mudrick, Harry 84
Murray, Mary 58
Murray, Maureen 47, 58

N

NAACP 33, 44, 49, 52, 58, 67, 77, 85, 90, 93, 95, 114, 122, 129, 163

Nacrelli, John 131, 133, 144, 159
Nails, John 150
National Corp of Housing Partnership 141
National Urban League 89
Negro Women's Business and Professional Club 151
Nelson, Emory O. 70
New Alliance Party 154
"New Negro" 51, 72, 84
Nichols, Jim 79
Ninth Ward 74
Norris, Herbert "Stardust" 65
Norris, J. Austin 37
Nugent Court 20
Nugent, George 17
Nugent, Lorenzo 17
NYA 44, 67

O

Odd Fellows Lodge 22
OIC (Opportunities Industrialization Center) 52, 138
O'Rourke, Vernon 88

P

Page, Clarence 164
Parker, John and Mary 18
Parker, William 134
Patrick, Rev. H. R. 52
Pendergast, Tom 29
Penn housing project 75, 90, 137, 148
Penn Morton College 104
Pennsylvania Crime Commission 159, 165
Pennsylvania Department of Labor 145
Pennsylvania Department of Public Instruction 123
Pennsylvania Human Relations Commission 122, 124
Pennsylvania Military College 104, 144
Pennsylvania Utilities Commission 77
Penn, William 15
Peoples, Cliff 90

Index

Pew, J. Newton 123
Pew, John 67, 88
Philadelphia Afro-American (newspaper) 82
Philadelphia Independent (newspaper) 68
Philadelphia Tribune (newspaper) 43, 95, 121, 167
Pipes, Carrie M. 39, 62
Pittsburgh Courier (newspaper) 43, 70, 88
Plafker, Nathaniel 119
Polish-American Club 147
Polish National Alliance 130
"Popper Stopper" 39
Powell, Jessie 48, 136
Presbyterians 22
Purnsley, Ellery 76, 92, 104
Purnsley, Merritt (Buddy) 18

Q

Quakers 15, 16, 17, 22, 89, 109, 140

R

Rainey, Joseph H. 37, 95
Range, Elder Cornelius 53
Raymond, George T. 44, 54, 84, 90, 102, 108, 115, 154
Reading, Albert A. 27, 34, 104
Reading, Edgar Richardson 32
Reading, Lester 34, 82
Reading, Russell 78
Reading, Samuel Sr. 34
Reason, John F. L. 72
Reed, Arthur 21
Reed, John 76
Reed, Judge Howard 151
Reynolds, Hobson R. 37
Reynolds Metal Co. 125
Rhodes, E. Washington 95
Richardson, Gloria 118, 119
Richardson, Jack 35
Richardson, J. Allen 35

181

Richardson, Leroy 35, 76, 91
Riley, Bill 133, 150
Riot, summer of 1917 23
Roberts, Clarence 120, 124, 135
Roberts, Theodore 77
Robeson, Paul 39
Robinson, Ollie 66
Robinson, Sugar Ray 41
Rouse, Dr. Felder, Jr. 130, 141
Royal African Company 15
Rutledge, Borough of 108

S

Sallard, Joseph 48
Savage, Philip 122
Schapp, Gov. Milton 130
Schools of Chester
  Chester High 43, 49, 58, 64, 98, 103, 110, 135, 152, 154, 155, 158
  Dewey-Mann 95, 103
  Douglass, Frederick 31, 57, 98
  Franklin 95, 104, 124
  Gartside 57
  Harvey 57
  Hoskins 57
  Jones 57, 98, 103
  Smedley 58, 95, 98
  Washington, Booker T. 31, 104
  Watts 18, 27, 57, 93, 97
Scott, Emmett J. 68
Scott Paper Co. 107, 123, 125, 158
Scott, Rev. Daniel A. 34, 50, 51, 93, 95, 138, 167
Scranton, Gov. William 122
Sharpe, Jimmie 134, 151
Shepherd, Rev. Marshal, Jr. 51
Shepherd, Rev. Marshal, Sr. 37
Shields, Lonnie 39
Sims, Bishop D. H. 69
Smith, Harold 48, 136
Spain, Charles 83, 104

Index

Sproul, Pennsylvania governor 39
Start, Raymond R. 106
Stinson Towers 138
Strand Theater 87
Student Non-violent Coordinating Committee (SNCC) 121
Sun Center 156
Sun Oil Co. 31, 68, 70, 77
Sun Shipyard 31, 67, 69, 77, 125, 144
Swarthmore College 104, 119, 158
Swarts, Ralph 90
Sweney, Judge Henry G. 91, 97, 105, 107, 130
Swiggett, Charles 103

T

Tent Sisters 22
Thomas, Elise 46
Thomas, Evola 45
Thomas, Rev. Thomas M. 20, 52
Thomas, Richard 38, 71, 100, 162
Thornburg, Richard 145
Trimble, Ike 41
Tucker, Lorenzo 40
Turpin, Oliver 38

U

Underground Railroad 16
Uniform Crime Report 148
Upper Chichester Borough 108, 141
US 39th Infantry, Colored Troops 17
USO Building 73

V

Valentine, William K. 39, 59
Van Roden, Judge Leroy 106
Vaul, John 136

W

Wade, Robert neighborhood house 17, 107, 140

183

War Board 30, 114, 129, 144, 163
Waters, Ethel 18
Watkins, Russ 88
Watson, Rufus 95, 97
Watts, Ellis 17
Watts, John 17, 26
Weaver, Robert C. 76
Wesley House 157
West Chester State College 39, 104
West End Ministerial Fellowship 52, 122, 138
West End YMCA 52, 70, 72, 99, 102, 157
Westinghouse Electric 159
West, Joseph S. 83, 104
Widener College 158
Widener University 104
Williams, John Francis 95, 97
Williams, Sherman 38
Willis, William 38
Wilson Day Nursery 26
Winters, Eva 121
Womack, David 158
Women's Christian Temperance Union 22
WPA 44, 67
Wricks, Lucy A. 48
Wright, Bishop R. R. 48
Wright, E. Courtlandt 21, 27, 32, 129
Wright, Perry A. 21, 35
Wright, Robert A. 35, 48, 109, 124, 129
Wright, Robert C. 130

Y

Yarnell Street 18
Yellow Cab Company 77
YMCA 96, 99, 102
York, Pennsylvania 145
YWCA 45, 102

Contributions of Richard E. Harris

Photos showing Richard Harris' involvement in providing opportunities for talented Black youth

Top: Harris with scholarship recipients. Middle: Scholarship committee. Bottom left: Harris with Black Writers' Workshop (1972). Bottom right: Dramatic skit with students.

Items from the collection of the George Washington Carver Museum and Cultural Center in Phoenix, which Richard Harris helped organize

Top: Old-time reporter's tools. Bottom left: A solider's sad farewell (W.W. I). Bottom right: Witch doll and African flags.

www.ingramcontent.com/pod-product-compliance
Ingram Content Group UK Ltd.
Pitfield, Milton Keynes, MK11 3LW, UK
UKHW021312180426
11947UKWH00015B/1171